DATE DUE

		MAY 0 2 2002
NOV 1 4 1995		FEB 0 2 2006
NOV 1 4 1995		FEB 1 4 2006
DEC 0 7 1995		
DEC 0 7 1995		
SEP 1 8 1997		
SEP 2 2 1997		
NOV 1 7 1997		
NOV 1 7 1997		
DEC 0 1 1997		
DEC 1 6 1997		
DEC 0 9 1997		
FEB 0 4 1998		
FEB 0 3 1998		
FEB 1 4 2006		

DOC
SHARON POLLOCK

Playwrights Canada
Toronto

DOC

Copyright © 1984 Sharon Pollock

PLAYWRIGHTS CANADA is the imprint of
PLAYWRIGHTS UNION OF CANADA
8 York Street, 6th Floor
Toronto, Ontario
Canada M5J 1R2
Phone (416) 947-0201

PLAYWRIGHTS UNION OF CANADA operates with the generous assistance
of the Canada Council, the Department of External Affairs, the
Ontario Ministry of Citizenship and Culture, the Ontario Arts
Council, Alberta Culture, Alberta Foundation for the Literary
Arts, Ontario-Quebec Permanent Commission, Wintario, the
Municipality of Metropolitan Toronto -- Cultural Affairs
Division, and the City of Toronto through the Toronto Arts
Council.

*Front cover photo: Michael Hogan in the 1984 Toronto Free
Theatre production of DOC.*
Front cover photo by Nir Bareket
Photo of Sharon Pollock by Don Johnson
Cover design by Lisa Dimson
Editor: Dave Carley

Canadian Cataloguing in Publication Data

Pollock, Sharon.
    Doc

A play.
ISBN 0-88754-448-7

I. Title

PS8581.043D62 1986   C812'.54   C86-093337-7
PR9199.3.P64D62 1986

First Edition: September 1986
Third printing: August 1988

Printed and bound in Canada

DOC was commissioned by Rick McNair, Theatre
Calgary, through the Doctor Betty Mitchell Fund,
and was first produced at that theatre in April
1984, with the following cast:

EV. . . . . .Michael Hogan

CATHERINE . . . . .Susan Hogan

KATIE . . . . Amanda Pollock

BOB . . . . Kate Trotter

OSCAR . . . . .Chuck Shamata

Directed by Guy Sprung

Designed by Terry Gunvordahl

Original Music and Sound Score by Allan Rae

Stage Manager - Laurie Champagne

DOC was extensively re-written and subsequently
produced by Toronto Free Theatre in September
1984, with the following cast changes:

CATHERINE . . . . .Clare Coulter

KATIE . . . . .Henriette Ivanans

There was also a new sound score by John Mills-
Cockell

The Characters:

EV: an elderly man in his 70's

CATHERINE: his daughter, in her mid-30's

KATIE: Catherine, as a young girl

BOB: Ev's wife, Catherine's mother

OSCAR: Ev's best friend

Playwright's Notes:

Much of the play consists of the sometimes shared, sometimes singular memories of the past, as relived by EV and CATHERINE, interacting with figures from the past. Structurally, shifts in time do not occur in a linear, chronological fashion, but in an unconscious and intuitive patterning of the past by EV and CATHERINE. A stage direction (Shift) marks these pattern changes which are often, but not always, time shifts as well. In production, music has been used to underscore the pattern shifts, however the characters' shifts from one pattern to another must be immediate. They do not "hold" for the music. The physical blocking must accommodate this immediacy and the stage setting facilitate it.

The "now" of the play takes place in the house in which CATHERINE grew up and in which EV now lives alone. The play is most effective when the set design is not a literal one, and when props and furniture are kept to a minimum. I think of the setting as one which has the potential to explode time and space while simultaneously serving certain naturalistic demands of the play.

A kaleidoscope of memory constitutes the dialogue and action of the opening sequence. It is followed by a scene set more firmly in the "now". EV is

"old" during these two segments, as he is at the
opening and closing of Act Two. Although EV
relives the past as a younger man, we never see
CATHERINE any age but in her mid-thirties. She
is able to speak across time to her father, to her
mother, and to her younger self. CATHERINE and
KATIE blend, sharing a sense of one entity,
particularly in the scenes with her father's best
friend, OSCAR. This should not be interpreted to
mean that CATHERINE and KATIE share one mind or
are always in accord. They are often in conflict.

OSCAR is first seen in the opening sequence wearing
a Twenties-era hockey uniform. He is a young man
about to enter medical school. OSCAR's scenes with
KATIE cover a four year period prior to and ending
with BOB's death. In the scenes he shares with
BOB and EV there is a longer, more chronological
unfolding of time. For the most part, we see him
as a man in his mid-thirties.

We see BOB in her mid-twenties to mid-thirties.
She wears a dressing gown which has a belt or tie
at the waist, and under this she wears a slip.
The material of the gown is satin or satin-like;
the gown itself has the look of a tailored long
dinner gown when appropriately belted. On other
occasions, undone and flapping, it has the
appearance of a sloppy kimono. Is it necessary
to say that her descent into alcoholism, despair,
and self-disgust must be carefully charted?

EV as an old man wears glasses and a worn cardigan
sweater.

There are liquor bottles on stage in Act One; they
have been removed from the set in Act Two. A
trunk is useful on stage; it holds photos and
memorabilia; as well, it provides a storage place
in Act One for OSCAR's hockey uniform, and the
clothing into which he and EV will change.

In some productions all characters are always on
stage with the exception of EV, who is free to
exit and enter during the play, and KATIE, BOB,
and OSCAR who exit near the end of the play. In
other productions there has been a greater freedom
of movement re characters' exits and entrances.
The script indicates where a character "may enter"
or "may exit". If this is not indicated, the
character must remain on stage.

DOC

<u>Act One</u>

In the black there is a subtle
murmuring of voices, with the
odd phrase and word emerging
quite clearly. They are
repeats of bits and pieces of
dialogue heard later in the
play. The voices are those of
KATIE, OSCAR, BOB and the
young EV; they often speak on
top of each other.

Light grows on EV, who is
seated by the open trunk. He
holds an unopened letter. A
match flares as BOB lights a
cigarette in the background.
Light grows on BOB, on OSCAR
who is smoothing tape on his
hockey stick, and on KATIE who
concentrates on moving one foot
back and forth slowly and
rhythmically. EV slowly closes
the trunk, his focus still on
the envelope he holds.

CATHERINE enters. She carries
an overnight bag as well as her

> shoulder bag. She puts the
> overnight bag down. She sees
> KATIE. She watches KATIE for
> a moment, and then speaks to
> KATIE's rhythmic movement.

CATHERINE: Up-on the carpet...you shall kneel...
            while the grass...grows in the field

> (KATIE's motion turns into
> skipping as KATIE turns an
> imaginary skipping rope and
> jumps to it)

            Stand up straight
            Upon your feet

KATIE: (speaks with CATHERINE. The murmuring
            of voices can still be heard but they
            are fading)
            Choose the one you love so sweet
            Now they're married wish them well
            First a girl, gee that's swell

> (KATIE's voice is growing louder,
> taking over from CATHERINE)

KATIE &
CATHERINE: Seven years after, seven to come

KATIE: (alone)
            Fire on the mountain kiss and run
            (jumps "pepper" faster and faster)
            Tinker, tailor, soldier, sailor,
            Rich man, poor man, beggar man thief

BOB: Doctor

KATIE: Doc-tor!!! (stops skipping)

CATHERINE: (removing her gloves) Daddy?

EV: (looks up from the envelope) Katie?
               (stands up) Is that you, Katie?

KATIE: (skipping towards EV singing) La da
               da da daah.

                    (KATIE continues her "la dahs"
                    skipping away from EV as OSCAR
                    speaks)

OSCAR: Hey, you and me, Ev.

                    (EV looks at the letter and sits
                    back down)

               Best friends. Ev and Oscar, Oscar
               and Ev - and if we weren't - I
               think I'd hate you.

KATIE: (stops skipping but continues) La
               dada da daah

BOB: Why don't you open it?

OSCAR: You see, Ev - you're just too good
               at things.

BOB: Go on, open it.

                    (the murmuring voices have faded
                    out)

OSCAR: It makes people nervous.

                    (sound of an approaching train
                    whistle)

               It makes me nervous.

BOB: Listen.

(The train whistle is growing in
volume. KATIE stops her "la da
da dahs")

Your Gramma, Katie, his mother. She'd
set her clock by that train. Set her
clock by the junction train crossing
the railway bridge into Devon. Must
be what? Three-quarters of a mile of
single track spanning the river? And
midnight, every night, that train
coming down from the junction -
half-way across three-quarters of a
mile of single track its whistle
would split the night...and that night
do you know what she did?

EV: (his focus on the letter) No.

BOB: She walked out to meet it.

EV: No.

BOB: You wanna know something, Katie?

KATIE: No.

BOB: Your father's mother, your grandmother,
               killed herself...Katie!

KATIE: What!

BOB: She walked across the train bridge at
               midnight and the train hit her.

KATIE: That's an accident.

BOB: She left a letter, and the letter tells
               him why she did it.

KATIE: There isn't any letter.

BOB: What's that?

KATIE: Daddy?

BOB: And he won't open it cause he's
             afraid, he's afraid of what she
             wrote.

KATIE: Is that true, Daddy?

EV: No.

KATIE: Is that the letter?

EV: Your grandmother was walking across
             the Devon bridge-

KATIE: What for?

EV: Well - it was a kind of short cut.

BOB: Short cut?

EV: And she got caught in the middle of a
             span and she was hit and killed.

CATHERINE: I stayed with her once when I was
             little...I can hardly remember.

EV: (continuing to talk to KATIE) It was
             after your mother had Robbie.

KATIE: Why didn't I stay with you and Robbie
             and Mummy?

EV: Your mother was sick so you stayed
             with your Gramma.

CATHERINE: Yes...and she made me soft-boiled runny eggs, and she'd feed me them and tell me stories about Moses in the bullrushes, and I...and I...would peel the wallpaper off behind the door, and she'd get angry.

EV: That's right.

CATHERINE: Why didn't she jump?

OSCAR: A hat trick Ev! Everybody screaming - everybody on their feet - what's it feel like, Ev?

BOB: He doesn't care. He doesn't care about anything except his "prac-tice" and his "off-fice" and his "off-fice nurse" and all those stupid, stupid people who think he's God.

EV: (to KATIE) Don't listen to her.

BOB: You're not God.

EV: Your mother's sick.

KATIE: No she isn't.

OSCAR: God, you're good. You fly, Ev.

KATIE: Why do you keep saying she's sick?

OSCAR: You don't skate, you fly.

KATIE: She's not sick.

EV: Your mother's -

KATIE: Why do you keep saying that!

EV: Katie –

KATIE: No!

CATHERINE: For a long time I prayed to God. I
                 asked him to make her stop. I prayed
                 and prayed. I thought, I'm just a
                 little girl. Why would God want to
                 do this to a little girl? I thought
                 it was a mistake. I thought maybe he
                 didn't know. I don't know what I
                 thought. I prayed and prayed... Now,
                 I don't believe in God.

KATIE: And if there is a God, then I don't
                 like him.

EV: She isn't well.

                 (BOB slowly opens a drawer, feels
                 inside it, and runs her hand
                 along a chair cushion. She
                 continues to quietly,
                 unobtrusively look for something
                 as KATIE and EV speak)

KATIE: Tell Robbie that. He wants to believe
                 that. I want the truth.

EV: I'm telling you the truth.

KATIE: No! Do you know what I did yesterday?
                 She kept going to the bathroom and
                 going to the bathroom and I went in
                 and looked all over and I found it.
                 In the clothes hamper with all the
                 dirty clothes and things. And I took
                 it and I poured it down the sink and
                 I went downstairs and I threw the
                 empty bottle in the garbage so don't
                 tell me she's sick!

BOB: It's gone.

               (BOB looks at KATIE. In the
               following sequence, although
               CATHERINE is the speaker, BOB
               will act out the scene with KATIE)

CATHERINE: No. No, don't.

BOB: It's gone.

CATHERINE: No.

BOB: You.

CATHERINE: No.

BOB: You took it and I want it back.

               (BOB grabs KATIE)

               I want it back!

CATHERINE: It's gone now and you can't have it.

BOB: Where? You tell me where?

CATHERINE: I poured it out.

BOB: No.

CATHERINE: Down the sink.

BOB: No.

CATHERINE: It's gone, forget it.

BOB: It's mine, I want it back!

CATHERINE: Gone.

BOB: No fair!

                (BOB struggles with KATIE)

CATHERINE: Let me go!

BOB: No right!

CATHERINE: Let me go!

BOB: You had no right!

                (KATIE strikes BOB, knocking her
                down)

CATHERINE: Daddy!

EV: Katie?

                (EV gets up from his chair and
                moves to look for CATHERINE.
                OSCAR may follow him. EV does
                not see CATHERINE, nor she him)

OSCAR: You know my father wishes I were you.
                He does. He wishes I were you.
                "Oscar," he says, "Oscar, look at Ev
                - why can't you be like Ev."

BOB: Look at what your father did.

KATIE: You lie.

OSCAR: I say nothing. There's nothing to be
                said. "You got to have that killer
                instinct on the ice," he says. I play
                goalie - what the hell's a killer
                instinct in a goalie? Then he says,
                "Oscar," he says, "Oscar, you are
                goin' into medicine."

10

EV: Katie?

OSCAR: My Dad's a doctor so I gotta be a
               doctor.

BOB: Your father hit me and I fell.

KATIE: You're always lying.

BOB: See?

KATIE: He didn't hit you.

BOB: See?

KATIE: I hit you! - Get away from me!

OSCAR: What's so funny is you're the one so
               bloody keen on medicine - you'd kill
               for medicine. (laughs) Hey Ev, kill
               for medicine, eh. (laughs)

BOB: Your father's mother, your Gramma,
               killed herself and he's afraid to open
               it.

KATIE: (covers her ears) Now they're married
                 wish them joy
               First a girl for a toy
               Seven years after, seven to come,
               Fire on the mountain, kiss and run

                   (EV returns from his search for
                   CATHERINE. OSCAR follows him.
                   KATIE sees CATHERINE, and moves
                   towards her, speaking the verse
                   to her)

KATIE: On the mountain berries sweet
               Pick as much as you can eat

By the berries bitter bark
Fire on the mountain break your heart

KATIE &
CATHERINE: Years to come - kiss and run -
bitter bark -

    (CATHERINE sees EV, who sees
    CATHERINE. CATHERINE speaks
    softly, almost to herself)

CATHERINE: Break your heart...
...It's me, Daddy.

EV: Katie?

KATIE: When I was little, Daddy.

CATHERINE: It's Catherine now, call me Catherine
...well...aren't you going to say
anything?

EV: You're home.

CATHERINE: Ah-huh...a hug, a big hug, Daddy,
come on.

    (CATHERINE and EV embrace)

Ooh.

EV: What.

CATHERINE: How long has it been?

EV: Be ah...

CATHERINE: Four years, right? Medical convention
in where? Vancouver, right?

EV: That's right. Vancouver.

CATHERINE: Montreal, Toronto, Calgary, Van, where
               haven't we met, eh?

EV: Here.

CATHERINE: Yup. Not...not met here.

                    (CATHERINE notices the envelope
                     in EV's hand)

               What're you doing with that?

EV: Oh - just goin' through things.
               Clearin' things out.

                    (CATHERINE, getting out a
                     cigarette, turns away from EV)

BOB: Katie's afraid of what she wrote.

KATIE: (to CATHERINE) Is that true?

EV: Are you here for this hoopla tomorrow?

CATHERINE: Not really.

EV: There's gonna be speeches and more
               speeches. I lay the cornerstone, and
               dinner I think.

CATHERINE: Ah-huh.

EV: I got it all written down with the
               times.

CATHERINE: Ah-huh.

EV: I got it downstairs... You wanna take
               a look? ...Not here for that, eh.

CATHERINE: No. I came home to see you.

EV: Pretty sad state of affairs when your own daughter's in town and can't attend a sod-turnin' in honour of her father.

CATHERINE: So I'll go, I'll be there.

EV: Coulda sent a telegram, saved the air fare.

CATHERINE: Christ Daddy, don't be so stupid.

EV: Sound like your mother.

CATHERINE: I learnt the four letter words from you.

EV: Bullshit.

CATHERINE: I said I'd go, I said I'd be there. So. (pause) I'm proud of you, Daddy.

EV: Did you know it was a write-in campaign?

CATHERINE: Oh?

EV: The niggers from Barker's Point, the mill workers from Marysville, they're the ones got this hospital named after me. Left to the politicians God knows what they'd have called it.

CATHERINE: Well, I'm proud.

EV: Some goddamn French name I suppose - what?

CATHERINE: Proud, you must be proud having the hospital named after you.

14

EV: The day I first started practice, that
               day I was proud. Was the day after
               you were born... There was a scarlet
               fever epidemic that year, you remember?

CATHERINE: No Daddy.

EV: Somebody...some couple came in, they
               were carryin' their daughter, what
               was she? Two, maybe three? I took
               her in my arms...could see they'd left
               it too late. I remember that child.
               I passed her back to her mother. Hold
               her tight, I said. Hold her tight
               till she goes... Do you remember that
               woman holdin' that child in the hallway?

CATHERINE: No Daddy.

EV: No. That was your mother...that was
               your mother.

BOB: Blueberries, Katie.

EV: You were just little then.

BOB: Blueberries along the railway tracks,
               and every year we'd pick them and sell
               them. I was the youngest, and Mama
               was always afraid I'd get lost, but
               I never got lost.

                    (CATHERINE looks at BOB)

               Not once.

                    (Pause)

EV: What are you thinkin'?

CATHERINE: (looks away from BOB) Nothing...You've
              lost weight.

EV: Of course I lost. I damn near died.
              You didn't know that, did you.

CATHERINE: No. No, nobody told me.

EV: Well it was that goddamn heart man.
              It was him gave me a heart attack.

CATHERINE: Really?

EV: What the hell's his name?

CATHERINE: Whose?

EV: The heart man's!

CATHERINE: I wouldn't know, Daddy.

EV: Demii - no, Demsky. I go to him, I
              tell him I been gettin' this pain in
              my ticker, and he has me walkin' up
              and down this little set a stairs,
              and runnin' on treadmills. Jesus
              Christ, I said to him, I'm not tryin'
              out for a sports team, I'm here because
              I keep gettin' this pain in my ticker!
              For Christ's sake, I said, put a
              stethoscope to my chest before you kill
              me with these goddamn stairs!

CATHERINE: So how are you now?

EV: It would've served the bastard right if
              I'd died right there in his office -
              do you remember how good Valma was
              with your mother?

CATHERINE: I remember.

EV: Every statutory holiday your mother's killin' herself or seein' things crawlin' on the walls or some goddamn thing or other, and Valma is like a rock, isn't that right?

CATHERINE: I guess so.

EV: So I come home from Demsky's, and I get the pain in my ticker and I wait all night for it to go away, and long about four or four-thirty, I phone Valma. Valma, I say, I'm havin' a heart attack, Valma - and she drops the phone nearly breakin' my ear drum and I can't phone out and I'm damned if I'm gonna get in that car and die all alone on Charlotte Street like that foolish Hazen Arbeton - If you were livin' in town, I'd have phoned you.

CATHERINE: You couldn't if Valma dropped the phone, Daddy.

EV: I'd have phoned you first!

CATHERINE: Would you?

EV: Well if I'd known she was gonna drop that goddamn phone I would have.

CATHERINE: What about Robbie?

EV: Who?

CATHERINE: Your son - Robbie.

EV: I'm not senile, I know who the hell Robbie is, what about him?

CATHERINE: You could have phoned him.

EV: I couldn't phone anyone! I was connected to Valma and I couldn't get disconnected!

CATHERINE: Would you have phoned him if you could?

EV: He wouldn't be home.

CATHERINE: How do you know?

EV: He's never home.

CATHERINE: Do you see him much?

EV: How the hell could I if he's never home?

CATHERINE: Do you try to see him!

EV: Of course I try! Have you seen him, phoned him, been over to visit?

CATHERINE: For Christ's sake Daddy, I just got in.

EV: Do you write?

CATHERINE: To Robbie?

EV: Yes to Robbie! You sure as hell don't write to me!

CATHERINE: I don't have the time.

EV: Some people make time.

CATHERINE: Why don't you?

EV: I'm busy.

CATHERINE: So am I.

EV: Mn. (pause) Does he ever write you?

CATHERINE: No.

EV: Do you wonder why?

CATHERINE: He's busy! Everyone's busy!

EV: Bullshit. It's that woman of his.

CATHERINE: It isn't.

EV: Paula.

CATHERINE: Who's Paula?

EV: She thinks we're all crazy.

CATHERINE: Well maybe we are, who in hell's Paula?

EV: His wife!

CATHERINE: You mean Corinne.

EV: What did I say?

CATHERINE: You said Paula.

EV: Well I meant Corinne! (pause) Paula. Who the hell's Paula? (pause)

BOB: Pauline.

EV: Pauline now, that was a friend of your mother's. Died a cancer, died in your room, and where did you sleep?

CATHERINE: In this room

EV: because

CATHERINE: the maid had left

EV: and your mother nursed Pauline right
               through to the end. Didn't touch a
               drop for three months.

               (As CATHERINE turns away, she sees
               BOB)

BOB: Not a drop for three months, Katie.

               (Pause)

EV: Best...best office nurse...I - ever
               had.

CATHERINE: Who, Mummy?

EV: Not Mummy, no. Valma. She ran that
               office like Hitler rollin' through
               Poland, and good with your mother -

CATHERINE: (turns back to EV) I know, forty
               years like a rock.

EV: That's right, like a rock, but I call
               her with that heart attack, and she
               goes hysterical. I never saw that in
               her before. It was a surprise. It
               was a goddamn disappointment. She
               comes runnin' into the house and up the
               stairs and huffin' and puffin' and
               blue in the face and - I'm on the
               bathroom floor by this time. She sees
               that, and gets more hysterical. She's
               got to run next door - my phone not

workin' bein' connected to her phone
which she dropped breakin' my ear
drum - and she phones the hospital.
And then we sit - I lie, she sits -
and we wait for the goddamn ambulance,
her holdin' my hand and bawlin'.

CATHERINE: Poor Valma.

EV: Poor Valma be damned! If I'd had the
strength I'd have killed her. I kept
tellin' her two things, I said it
over and over - one, you keep that
Demsky away from me - and you know
what she does?

CATHERINE: She is sixty-seven.

EV: I'm seventy-three, you don't see me
goin' hysterical! And I'm the one
havin' the heart attack!

CATHERINE: Alright.

EV: You know the first thing I lay eyes
on when I wake up in that hospital
bed? Well, do you!

CATHERINE: No, I don't know, no.

EV: First thing I see is that goddamn
Demsky hangin' over me like a vulture.
Demsky who gave me the heart attack!
...Next death bed wish I make I sure
as hell won't make it to Valma.

CATHERINE: Well...it wasn't a real death bed wish,
Daddy. You're still here.

EV: No thanks to her!

(Pause)

CATHERINE: So?

EV: So what?

CATHERINE: Jesus Daddy, so how are you now?

EV: I don't read minds, I'm not a mind-reader!

CATHERINE: How are you!

EV: I'm fine!

CATHERINE: Good.

EV: What?

CATHERINE: I said good. Great. I'm glad that you're fine.

EV: Got the nitro pills...pop a coupla them. Slow down they say. Don't get excited, don't talk too fast, don't walk too fast, don't, don't, don't, just pop a pill.

CATHERINE: Is it hard?

EV: Is what hard?

CATHERINE: Is it hard to slow down?

EV: ...The nurses could always tell when I'd started my rounds. They could hear my heels hittin' the floor tiles, hear me a wing away.

              (OSCAR starts to laugh quietly)

                    Did I ever tell you...

OSCAR: That's what you call a Cuban heel, Ev.

EV: ...'Bout those white woman's shoes I
                bought on St. Lawrence?

CATHERINE: For the O.R.

EV: That's right. They were on sale, real
                cheap, but they fit my foot cause my
                foot is so narrow.

OSCAR: Still, a woman's shoe, Ev?

EV: A good shoe for the O.R. was hard to
                find then!

CATHERINE: So you bought two pair.

EV: And I wore em. - How did you know?

CATHERINE: You told me.

EV: I told you.

CATHERINE: Don't you remember? You and Uncle
                Oscar would act that whole story out
                ...Do you see Uncle Oscar? (pause)
                Daddy? (pause) Well...anyway...so,
                what was the other thing?

EV: Mn?

CATHERINE: The other thing. You kept telling
                Valma two things, Demsky, and what
                was the other?

EV: Don't tell Katie. I musta said that a
                dozen times. I could hear myself.

You're not to tell Katie. You're not
to tell Katie.

CATHERINE: Why not?

EV: Because I didn't want you to know.

CATHERINE: Why not?

EV: Because I knew, even if you did know,
you wouldn't come - and my heart
would've burst from that pain.

> (CATHERINE and EV look at each
> other. CATHERINE looks away)

Look at me - look at me!...

> (CATHERINE looks at EV)

You knew. That goddamn Valma, she
told you.

CATHERINE: No -

EV: You think I don't know a lie when I
hear it, I see it, right in your
goddamn eyes I can see it.

CATHERINE: Alright, alright, Valma did write -

EV: Ignores every goddamn thing I tell
her.

CATHERINE: You could have died, Daddy.

EV: If you gave a damn you'd have been
here!

CATHERINE: I don't want to fight.

24

EV: You afraid?

CATHERINE: No.

EV: I'm not afraid.

CATHERINE: God.

EV: Looked death in the face in that
           goddamn bathroom. It's not easy
           starin' death down with Valma bawlin'
           beside you. Every bit a your bein'
           directed, concentrated on winnin',
           not lettin' go... (gets out nitro
           pills; unscrews top while talking;
           takes pill by placing it under his
           tongue during his speech) Hated,
           hated losin'! Always. Hockey,
           politics, surgery, never mattered to
           me, just had to win. Could never let
           go. Do you know...do you know I saved
           Billy Barnes' life by hangin' onto
           his hand? I would not let him go till
           the sulfa took hold. I hung onto his
           hand, and I said Billy, goddamn it,
           you fight! And he did. They said it
           was the sulfa that saved him, miracle
           drug in those days, but you could
           never convince Billy of that. "Goddamn
           it, Doc, it was you!"... I opened his
           belly two or three years ago. Opened
           his belly and closed his belly.
           Inoperable carcinoma... "Are you
           tellin' me this thing is gonna kill
           me, Doc?" I reached out my hand and
           he took it... Hung...onto my hand...

CATHERINE: I would have come, but you didn't want
           me to know.

EV: But you did know, didn't you. That goddamn Valma, she told you, and you didn't come.

CATHERINE: I'm here now.

EV: Bit of free time, drop in and see the old man, eh?

CATHERINE: No.

EV: But if his ticker gives out and catches you typin', too bad.

CATHERINE: Don't.

EV: So were you workin' or weren't you workin'?

CATHERINE: I'm always working.

EV: And that's more important than your own father.

CATHERINE: Don't start.

EV: A woman your age should be raisin' a family.

CATHERINE: What family did you ever raise? You were never home from one day to the next so who are you to talk to me about family?

EV: Your father, that's who. The one who damn near died with no one but an office nurse by his side.

CATHERINE: Valma loves you!

EV: That's not what we're talkin' about here. We're talkin' about you and your work and your father dyin', that's what we're talkin' about!

CATHERINE: Are we?

EV: That's what I'm talkin' about - I don't know what the hell you're on about - I don't know what the hell you're doin' here!

CATHERINE: I just came home to see you, I wanted to see you...have you got any idea how hard it was for me to come home, to walk in that door, to, to come home?... Have you?...and when I leave here...my plane...could fall out of the sky, you could get another pain in your ticker, we could never talk again...all the things never said, do you ever think about that?

EV: You mean dyin'?

CATHERINE: No, more than that, I mean...I don't know what I mean.

(Pause)

EV: Are you still with that...whatshisname?

CATHERINE: Sort of.

EV: What's his name?

CATHERINE: What's it matter, you never remember.

EV: What's his name? Dugan? or Dougan?

CATHERINE: That was before, years before, Daddy.

EV: You should get one and hang onto one, Katie. Then I'd remember.

CATHERINE: I...

EV: What?

CATHERINE: I said it's difficult to keep a relationship goin' when when you're busy, right?

EV: Why don't you marry this whosits?

CATHERINE: Yeah, well...Whosits talks about that.

EV: I'm still waitin' for a grandson you know.

CATHERINE: I'm too old for that.

EV: You're soon gonna be - how old are you anyway?

CATHERINE: Besides I'd only have girls.

EV: Robbie's got girls...girls are all right... You can have girls if you want.

CATHERINE: I said I don't know if I want.

EV: But get married first.

CATHERINE: Actually - I've been thinking...of... of maybe calling it quits with whosits.

EV: Quits?

CATHERINE: Ah-huh.

EV: You're callin' it quits.

CATHERINE: The work you know. Makes it hard.

EV: I thought this was the one. What the
               hell was his name, Sturgeon or Stefan
               or -

CATHERINE: His name doesn't matter.

EV: Stupid goddamn name - an actor, an
               actor for Christ's sake.

CATHERINE: We're not goin' to get into whosits
               and me and marriage and me and kids
               and me, all right?

EV: You go through men like boxes of
               kleenex.

CATHERINE: I don't want to talk about it!

EV: Jesus Christ, I can't keep up.

CATHERINE: No you can't! You can't even
               remember his name!

EV: Burgess Buchanan, that was his name!
               And you sat in the lounge at the
               Bayside and you said, "Oh Daddy, you
               just got to meet him, he's such a
               nice fella, he's so understanding,
               and he's so this and he's so that and
               he's..." So explain to me what went
               wrong this time?

CATHERINE: Why do we always end up yelling and
               screaming, why do we do that?

EV: I care 'bout you!... I want to see you settled, Katie. Happy. I want you to write, letters, not... I want you close.

CATHERINE: ...I do write somebody you know. I write Uncle Oscar...every once in a while...when the spirit moves me.

EV: Not often.

CATHERINE: No. Not often. But I do. Write letters to someone. I do make the time. I know you and he don't keep in touch any more but I like to.

EV: Not lately.

CATHERINE: No, not lately. I...why do you say that?

EV: He was fly-fishin'. He slipped and fell in the Miramichi with his waders on.

CATHERINE: (upset) No... Did - did you see him?

EV: At the morgue when they brought him in.

CATHERINE: I mean before. Did you see him before? Were the two of you talking?

    (EV shakes his head)

    Why not?

EV: Too late.

CATHERINE: Now it's too late.

EV: Too late even then. Even before. Too much had been said.

CATHERINE: I wish you'd have told me.

EV: Would you have come home for him?

CATHERINE: ...Probably not.

EV: So what difference does it make?

CATHERINE: I like to know these things. Whether I can come or not. I can't help it if I'm in the middle of things.

EV: You make sure you're always in the middle of something. It's an excuse. How old are you now?

CATHERINE: Stop asking me that.

EV: You're gonna end up a silly old woman with nothin' but a cat for company.

CATHERINE: It'll be a live-in cat which is more than you've got with Valma.

EV: If I wanted Valma here, she'd be here.

CATHERINE: So you don't want her here, eh? You like it alone. Sitting up here all alone!

EV: I am not alone!

CATHERINE: You and Robbie, the same city, you never see Robbie!

EV: Go on! Why doncha go on! You got so goddamn much to say, why don't you say it! I am alone and it's you left me alone! My own daughter walkin' out and leavin' her father alone!

CATHERINE: How many years before you noticed my bed wasn't slept in?

EV: Don't go pointin' your finger at me! Look at yourself! What the hell do you do? Work, work, work - at what, for Christ's sake?

CATHERINE: I write! I'm good at it!

EV: Writing, eh Katie?

CATHERINE: Don't call me Katie!

EV: I'll call you by the name we gave you and that name is Katie.

CATHERINE: It's Catherine now.

EV: Oh, it's Catherine now, and you write Literature, don't you? And that means you can ignore your brother and your father and dump this Buchanan jerk and forget kids and family, but your father who gave his life to medicine because he believed in what he was doin' is an asshole!

CATHERINE: I never said that!

EV: My whole family never had a pot to piss in, lived on porridge and molasses when I was a kid.

CATHERINE: Alright!

EV: And fought for every goddamn thing I got!

CATHERINE: And it all comes down to you sitting up here alone with Gramma's letter!

EV: I am goin' through things!

CATHERINE: Why won't you open it?

EV: I know what it says.

CATHERINE: Tell me.

EV: You want it, here, take it.

    (CATHERINE grabs letter from EV. She almost rips it open, but stops and turns it in her hand. Pause)

CATHERINE: Did Gramma really walk out to meet it?

EV: It was an accident.

CATHERINE: What was Mummy?

EV: You blame me for that.

CATHERINE: No.

EV: It was all my fault, go on, say it, I know what you think.

CATHERINE: It was my fault.

EV: Oh for Christ's sake!

    (EV moves away from CATHERINE. He sits, takes off his glasses and

                rubs the bridge of his nose. He
                looks at CATHERINE, then back to
                the glasses which he holds in his
                hand)

                ...Your mother...

CATHERINE: Yes?

EV: Your mother and I –

CATHERINE: Tell me. Explain it to me.

BOB: There were eight of us, Katie, eight
of us.

OSCAR: (softly) Go, go.

BOB: How did my mama manage?

                (OSCAR stands up, holding two
                hockey sticks. He is looking at
                EV, whose back is to him. EV
                puts his glasses in his pocket)

OSCAR: Go.

BOB: All older than me, all born before he
went to war.

OSCAR: Go.

BOB: Him, her husband, my father, your
grandfather, Katie.

OSCAR: Go. Go!

BOB: And her with the eight of us and only
the pension.

34

OSCAR: Go!! Go!!

BOB: How did my mama manage?

           (BOB may exit. Shift)

OSCAR: Go!!! Go!!!

           (OSCAR throws a hockey stick at
           EV who stands, turns, plucking
           it out of the air at the last
           minute. They are catapulted back
           in time, rough-housing after a
           game)

           Go!!! The Devon Terror has got the
           puck, out of his end, across the blue
           line, they're mixing it up in the
           corner and he's out in front, he
           shoots! He scores! Rahhhh!

           (OSCAR has ended up on the floor
           with his hockey sweater pulled
           over his head. EV, who's scored,
           raises his arms in acknowledgement
           of the crowd's "Rah!". EV helps
           OSCAR up)

           You know somethin' Ev? This is the
           truth. Honest to God. Are you
           listenin'?

EV: Yeah.

           (EV takes off his "old man"
           sweater and hangs it on the back
           of a chair. During the following
           dialogue, OSCAR changes out of
           his hockey clothes, putting them
           in the trunk. He removes a jacket,

>pants and shoes for EV, and a
>suit of clothes plus shoes for
>himself)

OSCAR: When I think of medicine I get sick.
Yeah. The thought of medicine makes
me ill. Physically ill. Do you think
that could be my mother in me?

>(EV slips out of his slippers and
>removes his pants. OSCAR will
>put the pants in the trunk)

EV: Maybe.

OSCAR: My father says it's my mother in me.
At least she had the good sense to get
out. Leaving me with him. How could
she do that?

EV: I dunno. (puts on suit jacket)

OSCAR: The old man calls her a bitch. And
now nuthin' for it but I got to go
into medicine.

EV: So tell him no.

OSCAR: I can't.

EV: Stand up to him.

OSCAR: I can't.

EV: Just tell him.

OSCAR: It'd break his heart.

EV: Shit Oscar, it's your life, you can't
think about that.

OSCAR: Yeah.

EV: You just gotta tell him what you really want to do...how does that look?

OSCAR: Great.

EV: Which is?

OSCAR: Which is what?

          (OSCAR throws EV a tie)

EV: What you really want to do.

OSCAR: Oh.

EV: What do you really want to do?

OSCAR: I dunno.

EV: Come on.

OSCAR: Live someplace where it's hot.

EV: Come onnn...

OSCAR: New Orleans, I'd like to live in New Orleans.

EV: Oscar —

OSCAR: How hot is New Orleans anyway?

EV: And do what — in New Orleans, Oscar?

OSCAR: Do what. I dunno. Something. Anything. Not medicine.

(OSCAR reties EV's tie for him)

EV: Look, if you're gonna tell your father you don't want to do what he wants you to do, you can't just say your life's ambition is to live someplace where it's hot.

OSCAR: What if it is?

EV: That is not gonna work, Oscar.

OSCAR: You're a lot like my Dad, Ev. The two of you. You're always...

EV: What?

OSCAR: Forging ahead.

EV: What's wrong with that? (puts on pants)

OSCAR: Nothing. Forging is fine. I admire forging, I do, I admire it. It's just - not for me, do you think that could be my mother in me?

EV: Forget your mother. Concentrate on what you're gonna tell your father - and New Orleans is out.

OSCAR: It's honest, don't I get points for honest?

EV: Belt?

OSCAR: No points for honest.

EV: Or suspenders?

OSCAR:	What's honest, honest is nothing, nobody wants honest.
EV:	Honest is good, New Orleans is bad, belt or suspenders?
OSCAR:	Belt.

(OSCAR throws EV a belt)

EV:	Thanks.
OSCAR:	It's not fair.
EV:	I don't wanna hear about fair.
OSCAR:	Right.
EV:	Face it, you're a lazy son of a bitch.
OSCAR:	I know.
EV:	You've got no drive.
OSCAR:	I know.
EV:	You've got no push.
OSCAR:	I know.
EV:	I worked my ass off last summer in construction, what did you do?
OSCAR:	I lay in the sun.
EV:	That's right.
OSCAR:	I'm a loser.
EV:	And a whiner.

OSCAR: Right. (pause)   Why are we friends?

EV: Eh?

OSCAR: I agree with everything you say, it's
           the truth, what can I say? So why
           are we friends? - I figure it's the
           car and the clothes.

               (EV puts on shoes. By the end of
                scene he is dressed in suit, tie
                and shoes)

EV: That's a pretty shitty thing to imply.

OSCAR: I wasn't implying, I was just wondering.

EV: You've got other qualities.

OSCAR: Name one.

EV: We grew up together.

OSCAR: Go on.

EV: So we've known each other for a long
           time.

OSCAR: Yeah.

EV: Since Grade One.

               (Pause)

OSCAR: Well I figure it's the car and the
           clothes and the fact the old man
           dotes on you.

EV: Jesus Oscar.

OSCAR: Everybody knows I'm just a -

EV: Don't whine!

OSCAR: I'm not whining. I'm analyzing!

EV: I'm tryin' to help, Oscar. Now you
          must have some ambition, some desire,
          something you're at least vaguely
          interested in, that you could propose
          to your father as a kinda alternative
          to medicine, eh?

OSCAR: You mean apart from New Orleans.

EV: That's what I mean.

OSCAR: My mother might have gone to New
          Orleans.

EV: Forget your mother! Alternative to
          medicine! Not New Orleans!

OSCAR: Algeria.

EV: Oscar!

OSCAR: I know.

EV: I try to look out for you and it's
          like pissing on a forest fire.

OSCAR: I'm telling you exactly how I feel.
          I don't have ambitions and desires
          and goals in life. I don't need 'em.
          My old man has my whole life mapped
          out for me and I know what I'm supposed
          to do. I'm supposed to read and
          follow the map. That's it.

(EV moves away from OSCAR)

EV: There is no wardrobe and no car and no amount of dotage from your old man that would compensate a person for putting up with you!

(Shift)

CATHERINE: Uncle Oscar?

(OSCAR looks at KATIE as if it was she who had spoken. KATIE holds her shoe out to him)

Fix my shoe.

KATIE: It's got about a million knots - but keep talking.

CATHERINE: I want to know everything.

OSCAR: Construction work in the summer, hockey in the winter, and when we went to McGill, they'd bring him home on the overnight train to play the big games, the important games - and that's how he paid his way through medical school.

KATIE: Keep talking.

OSCAR: My father was their family doctor - I was there at his house the night his brother George died from the influenza - and that left him, and his sister Millie and his Mum and Dad.

CATHERINE: My Gramma.

KATIE: What was she like?

OSCAR: Proper. United Church. Poor and
            proper.

            (OSCAR gives KATIE back her shoe)

            That's all I remember.

            (KATIE hits OSCAR with the shoe)

KATIE: Remember more!

OSCAR: I think your father got his drive from
            your Gramma and you get yours from him.

KATIE: Are you saying I'm like her?

OSCAR: In some ways perhaps.

KATIE: I would never walk across a train
            bridge at midnight!

OSCAR: You might.

KATIE: I would not!

OSCAR: Well it was an accident she -

KATIE: What do you mean I might!

OSCAR: It was a short cut.

KATIE: I'm not like her! I would never do
            that!

OSCAR: It wasn't anything she did.

KATIE: I'm too smart to do that!

OSCAR: It was just something that happened.

43

KATIE: You don't know! You don't know anything!

OSCAR: Katie —

KATIE: Get away from me!

CATHERINE: Stop.

(Shift)

EV: If you want to know about this crazy bastard — if you want to know about him — When I needed a friend at my back, in a fight, in a brawl? This silly son of a bitch in sartorial splendour has saved my ass more than once — and me his — I'm gonna tell you a story. Now listen — we used to drink at this hole in the wall, this waterin' hole for whores and medical students, eh? And we'd sit there and nurse a beer all night and chat it up with the whores who'd come driftin' in well after midnight, towards mornin' really, and this was in winter, freeze a Frenchman's balls off — and the whores would come in off the street for a beer and we'd sit there all talkin' and jokin' around. They were nice girls these whores, all come to Montreal from Three Rivers and Chicoutimi and a lotta places I never heard tell of, and couldn't pronounce. Our acquaintance was strictly a pub acquaintance, we students preferin' to spend our money on beer thus avoidin' a medical difficulty which intimacy with these girls would most

likely entail. So - this night we're
stragglin' home in the cold walkin'
and talkin' to a bunch a these whores,
and as we pass their house, they drop
off there up the steps yellin'
"Goo-night goo-night"...Bout a block
further on, someone says: "Where the
hell's Oscar?" Christ, we all start
yellin': "Where the hell's Oscar?
Oscar! Oscar!" Searchin' in gutters,
snowbanks and alleys, but the bugger's
gone, disappeared! Suddenly it comes
to me. Surer than hell he's so pissed
he's just followed along behind the
girls when they peeled off to go home,
and he's back there inside the cat
house. So back I go. Bang on the
door. This giant of a woman, uglier
than sin, opens it up. Inside is all
this screamin' and cryin' and poundin'
and I say: "Did a kinda skinny fella"
- and she says: "Get that son of a bitch
outa here!" "Where is he?" I say.
"Upstairs, he's locked himself in one
of the rooms with Janette! He's
killin' her for Christ's sake! She
takes me up to the room, door locked,
girl inside is screamin' bloody murder
and I can hear Oscar makin' a kinda
intent diabolical ahhhhhin' and
oohhhin' sound. "Oscar! Oscar! For
Christ's sake, open up!" The girl's
pleadin' with him to stop, beggin'
him, chill your blood to the bone to
hear her. And still that aaahhhhhin'!
and ooohhhhhhin'! Nothin' for it but
I got to throw myself at the door till
either it gives or my shoulder does.
Finally Boom! I'm in. I can see
Oscar is not. He's got Janette tied

to the bed, staked right out, naked
and nude. He's straddlin' her but
he's fully clothed, winter hat, scarf,
boots and all, and he's wieldin' his
blue anatomy pencil. He's drawin'
all of her vital organs, he's outlinin'
them on her skin with his blue anatomy
pencil. He's got her kidneys and her
lungs, her trachea and her liver all
traced out. Takes four of us to pull
him off — me and three massive brutes
who've appeared. Janette is so upset
they send her back to Rivière-du-Loup
for two weeks to recover, Oscar has to
turn pimp till he pays back the price
of the door, and everyone swears it's
the worst goddamn perversion and misuse
of a whore ever witnessed in Montreal
...what in God's name did you think
you were doin' that night?

> (OSCAR shrugs and smiles. EV is
> taking out a letter and opening
> it as he speaks)

Jesus Christ...silly bastard...

> (Shift)

It's from Mum...the old man's been
laid off.

OSCAR: She sound worried?

EV: She says go ahead with the Royal Vic.

OSCAR: The General would be closer to home.

EV: What good would that do?

OSCAR: I don't know.

EV: No money to be made in post-graduate
            work anywhere.

OSCAR: I thought moral support, you know,
          being close.

EV: The Vic's the best in the country.

OSCAR: I know that.

EV: Mum would probably kill me if I gave
          up the Royal Vic.

OSCAR: She definitely would. ...What about
          Millie?

EV: Millie?

OSCAR: Yeah.

EV: What about her?

OSCAR: I guess she could probably help out.
          Get a job.

EV: There's no jobs anywhere. Besides
          Millie's still in school.

OSCAR: Will she quit?

EV: What the hell do you want me to do?

OSCAR: I don't want you to do anything. I
          just wondered if Millie would quit
          school to help out at home, that's all.

EV: What the hell're you tryin' to say to
          me? Are you sayin' I should quit?

OSCAR: No, I just meant there are hospitals
          closer to home.

              (OSCAR may exit. EV calls after
              him)

EV: You can't be serious. The Vic's the
               best post-graduate training in the
               country. I've worked goddamn hard
               for it and I won't give it up - not
               for Mum if she asked me! Not for
               Millie! Not for anyone!

CATHERINE: But you did, Daddy.

               (EV looks at CATHERINE)

               You gave it up for her.

EV: If...if you could have seen her.

                   (Shift. BOB may enter. She
                   carries a music box)

BOB: He would step off the elevator -
               every nurse on the floor, "Yes Doctor"
               - "No Doctor" - "Is there anything
               else" dramatic pause, sighhhh, "I
               can do for you, Doctor?" Even Matron.
               Yes, Matron! And the goo-goo eyes -
               I remember the eyes.

EV: Do you know what they said?

CATHERINE: What did they say?

EV: Forget her, she is immune to the
               charms of the predatory male.

BOB: They were right.

EV: No fraternization between doctors and
               nurses on pain of dismissal.

CATHERINE: So why did you ask her?

EV: I -

BOB: He couldn't resist me - and I -

             (BOB passes CATHERINE the jewellery box to hold. BOB opens the box. It plays "Smoke Gets In Your Eyes". BOB takes out a pair of earrings and puts them on as she's speaking. The lid of the box remains up and the music box plays during the scene)

             I don't give a fig for regulation or rules, only ones I make myself. And if in the past I chose to observe that regulation, it was only because a suitable occasion to break it hadn't arisen.

EV: Be serious.

BOB: My goodness, here I am without two pennies to rub together, and I rush out and buy a new sweater for a bar date with you, and you don't call that serious?

EV: When our eyes first met over what?...a perforated ulcer, were you serious then?

BOB: Do you know how many floors my mama scrubbed for that sweater?

             ("Smoke Gets In Your Eyes" played by big band fades in)

CATHERINE: (closes jewellery box) Was she really like that?

49

EV: If you could have seen her.

                 (OSCAR may enter)

OSCAR: Why risk it?

EV: Wait till you meet her.

                 (EV moves towards BOB, who is
                 swaying to the music)

OSCAR: I don't need to meet her. For Christ's
                 sake, Ev, you're... Ev?... Ev!

                 (EV and BOB dance to a medley of
                 Thirties tunes. OSCAR watches,
                 drawn into that warm atmosphere.
                 EV and OSCAR take turns cutting
                 in on each other, as they ballroom
                 dance with BOB. They're all very
                 good dancers, and OSCAR is as
                 captivated as EV by BOB. OSCAR
                 dances with BOB. She is looking
                 over his shoulder at EV. Shift)

KATIE: (interrupts, a sudden scream) Stop
                 that! You stop it!

                 (The dancers stop; a soft freeze)

                 I know things! I can figure things
                 out!

                 (The soft freeze breaks. Shift)

OSCAR: Have you told your mother?

EV: Not yet.

OSCAR: She had her heart set on a specialist.

EV: She'll settle for a grandson.

CATHERINE: But that's not what you got, you got me.

(Shift)

KATIE: Why did he marry her?

OSCAR: He loved her.

KATIE: Why didn't you marry her?

OSCAR: She loved him.

KATIE: They didn't want to have me.

OSCAR: That isn't true.

KATIE: Did your mother want to have you?

(Shift)

BOB: Your mother, ooohhh, your poor father, Ev.

EV: I know.

BOB: And Millie - you never told me about Millie.

EV: I mentioned her once or twice.

BOB: If you were only Catholic she could be a nun.

EV: Don't judge her by what you've seen
tonight.

BOB: And your mother could be Pope.

EV: She liked you.

BOB: She hated me.

EV: When you get to know her, it'll be
different.

BOB: I don't want to know her. Look at
Millie under her thumb.

EV: Millie isn't under her thumb.

BOB: And your father.

                (There is a sense of intimacy,
                rather than irritation, between
                EV and BOB)

EV: Look, you saw them for the first time
for what - four or five hours - you
can't make generalizations based on
that.

BOB: You were there. You heard her. "Poor
Ev. Giving up the Vic." You'd think
a general practice was the end of the
earth - And why've you fallen so far?

EV: She never said any of those things.

BOB: She implied I'd caught you by the
oldest trick in the book.

EV: She didn't.

BOB: "Why does a girl go into nursing?"
         Why to marry a doctor of course! And
         Millie nodding away and your father
         smiling away - I wanted to stand up
         and scream.

EV: You're tired.

BOB: And you, you're there, way up there,
         the shining light, can do nothing
         wrong, except one thing is wrong, we
         are wrong!

EV: She had certain expectations, I'm not
         defending her, I'm just trying to
         explain how things are, or have been
         - Bob?... Bob!

BOB: For years she's been practising, "I'd
         like you to meet my son, The Specialist."

EV: Things haven't been easy, you know.
         You've seen Dad, he's a good man but
         he's - when Georgie died, the old man
         wept on her - there was no one for her
         to weep on. It was hard on her losin'
         Georgie, and now all of her hopes for
         me and for Georgie are all pinned on
         me... You can understand that.

BOB: She'll be counting the months.

EV: Let her.

              (EV kisses BOB)

         Again.

              (EV kisses BOB)

         Again.

BOB: You.

EV: You smile that smile at my Mum and
            she'll love you. It's a beautiful
            smile.

BOB: We aren't wrong, are we?

EV: We'll have a boy and we'll call him
            George after my brother. She'll like
            that.

BOB: Or William, after my brother Bill.

EV: And he'll have a beautiful smile.

BOB: And he'll have a nose like yours.

EV: And he'll...

            (Shift. EV and BOB may exit)

CATHERINE: I notice this thing about having
            boys first. I mean what is that all
            about?

KATIE: Who was I named after?

OSCAR: Kate was your grandmother's name.

KATIE: Nobody calls me Kate.

OSCAR: That's your name.

KATIE: It's an ugly name. Why did they call
            me that? Couldn't they think of
            anything else?

OSCAR: Kate isn't ugly.

KATIE: Do I look like a Kate to you?

OSCAR: What's a Kate look like?

KATIE: Do you think names are like dogs?

OSCAR: In what way like dogs?

KATIE: I read dogs start to look like their
            owners or owners start to look like
            their dogs. Do you think if you get
            an ugly name you start to look like
            your name?

CATHERINE: Or be like who you were named
            after?

            (Shift. EV and BOB may enter.
            BOB carries EV's suitcoat. EV
            carries a doctor's bag. BOB will
            help EV on with his jacket)

BOB: I want to go back to work.

EV: Where would you work?

BOB: I'm an R.N., I'll apply at the
            hospital.

EV: No.

CATHERINE: Why not?

EV: I don't want her there.

CATHERINE: Why not?

EV: A matter of policy.

CATHERINE: Whose?

EV: What about Katie?

BOB: What about her?

EV: You should be home with her.

BOB: Why?

EV: You're her mother.

BOB: You're her father, you're not home
           from one day to the next. What am I
           supposed to do, rattle around with a
           four-month-old baby to talk to?

EV: So get somebody in.

BOB: Let me work, Ev.

EV: I don't want you down at the hospital.

BOB: Why not?

EV: Because as a surgeon operating out of
           that hospital, I don't want my wife on
           staff. I don't want any surgeon's
           wife on staff. And I don't know any
           surgeon who wants his wife on staff.

                (Shift)

KATIE: They were fighting last night.

OSCAR: Oh?

KATIE: Do you want to know what they were
           fighting about, if you don't already
           know.

OSCAR: How would I know?

KATIE: How do you think! Someone would
            tell you! Behind Daddy's back they
            would tell you! They would whisper.

OSCAR: That doesn't happen.

CATHERINE: Then why, Uncle Oscar, did you spend
            so much time talking to me if you
            didn't want to find out about them?

            (Shift)

BOB: I could work at the office. (pours
            herself a drink)

EV: No.

BOB: McQuire's wife —

EV: is a silly bitch who keeps McQuire's
            office in an uproar from the time she
            comes in in the morning till she leaves
            at night.

BOB: I'm not Marg McQuire.

EV: I have an office nurse, she does a
            good job and she needs the job and I
            don't intend letting her go.

BOB: I could work for somebody else!

EV: I don't know what doctor would hire
            another doctor's wife as an office
            nurse.

BOB: Why not?

EV: Look, you're not just an R.N. anymore.

BOB: No.

EV: You're not Eloise Roberts, you're not
            Bob any more.

BOB: Who am I?

EV: My wife.

CATHERINE: Daddy.

EV: She's working the O.R., the surgeon
            hits a bleeder, starts screaming for
            clamps, she's slow off the mark, and
            when the whole fuckin' mess is under
            control, he turns round to give her
            shit, she takes off her mask and who
            does he see? Not a nurse, another
            surgeon's wife. My wife. Is he gonna
            give her shit?

BOB: I'm not slow off the mark in the O.R.

EV: That's not the point, you're my wife,
            is he gonna give you shit?

BOB: That's his problem, not mine.

EV: I'm in the O.R. I hit a bleeder. I
            scream for a clamp. I look at the
            nurse who's too fuckin' slow and who
            do I see? My wife!

BOB: I'm not slow! I'm good in the O.R.

EV: That's not the point.

CATHERINE: Why don't you just say you don't want
            her there instead of all this bullshit?

EV: Jesus Christ I said it! I don't
              want her there!

                   (Shift. KATIE is holding her
                   wrist. She speaks to OSCAR)

KATIE: My father works hard! My father works
               really hard!

CATHERINE: I know. I know.

KATIE: You don't work as hard as my father.
               My father is never home. He goes to
               the hospital before we're up, and when
               he comes home we're asleep.

CATHERINE: Robbie's asleep.

KATIE: I'm surprised Daddy knows who Robbie
               is. I'm surprised Robbie knows who
               Daddy is... I hate Robbie.

OSCAR: How did this happen?

KATIE: I dunno.

OSCAR: Yes you do.

KATIE: I'm accident-prone. Some people are
               you know. Accident-prone. I do
               dangerous things. I like doing
               dangerous things.

OSCAR: How'd you do this?

KATIE: It was just something that happened.

OSCAR: Ah-huh.

                   (OSCAR is taping KATIE's wrist)

KATIE: I do lots of things. Last Sunday when we were supposed to be in Sunday School, Robbie and I, do you know what we did?

OSCAR: Might hurt.

KATIE: Won't hurt. We went to the freight yards and played. I crawled under the train cars twice and Robbie crawled over where they're hitched together. He was too scared to crawl under. I wasn't scared.

OSCAR: You shouldn't do that.

KATIE: We decided together, Robbie and I. I didn't make him. Do you believe that?

OSCAR: What?

KATIE: That Robbie and I decided together to go to the freight yards instead of to Sunday School, do you believe that?

OSCAR: No.

KATIE: Anyway we had these gloves on. You know the ones Mummy made out of kid or leather the last time she was away? She made about a million pair. She probably gave a pair to you.

(Shift)

BOB: It's not my fault if other people don't know who I am! It's not my fault if all they can see is your wife!

EV: Aren't you my wife?

BOB: That's not all I am!

EV: Don't yell at me.

BOB: Who do I yell at?

EV: Half the nurses in that goddamn hospital are lookin' for a doctor to marry so they can sit on their ass, and here you are screamin' cause you're not on your feet twelve hours a day bein' overworked and underpaid.

BOB: I am on my feet twelve hours a day!

EV: So let me get somebody in.

BOB: I feel funny with somebody in... If I'm here, I feel I should be doing it.

EV: You want to get out more.

BOB: I know I'm a good nurse. I'm as good as anyone. When I'm out... I'm never sure which fork to use.

EV: Who gives a shit which fork you use? Whichever one comes to hand.

BOB: When you "go out" that fork's important.

EV: Get Oscar to teach you how to play bridge. First year of university that's all he did.

BOB: I feel as if I wasted something.

(Shift. KATIE is still with
OSCAR)

KATIE: I don't know how she's supposed to get
            better by making gloves and painting
            pictures. Her pictures are awful.
            It costs a fortune to send her there
            and it never works!... Anyway...I
            got black all over my gloves and it
            wouldn't come off so I made Robbie
            give me his cause Mummy never gets
            mad at him and that's one of the
            reasons I hate him, and as soon as we
            got home do you know what he did?

CATHERINE: Told.

KATIE: He told. He said I <u>made</u> him go to
            the freight yards and then I <u>made</u> him
            change gloves. He's always telling
            and that's another reason I hate him.

OSCAR: You're the oldest - you should look
            out for Robbie.

KATIE: I am trying to teach Robbie to look
            out for <u>himself</u>! I am!... She didn't
            even ask and he told. She's always
            saying Robbie's just like her side of
            the family and I'm just like Daddy's -
            Have you met my Uncle Bill?

OSCAR: I might have.

KATIE: Well I wouldn't want to be like her
            side of the family. I'd rather be
            like his!

            (Shift)

BOB: Nobody else in my family finished
           high school, did I tell you that?

           (No one is listening to BOB)

CATHERINE: Was she a good nurse, Daddy?

EV: That's not the point, Katie.

CATHERINE: Was she?

EV: I'm late for my rounds.

BOB: I was the smartest.

EV: You get some sleep now.

           (EV may exit)

CATHERINE: Daddy?

BOB: And I always won, Katie! Because I
           played so hard! Played to win! And
           school - first, always first! "Our
           valedictorian is Eloise Roberts."

           (CATHERINE moves away from BOB,
           who continues speaking with the
           drink in her hand)

           Eloise Roberts, and they called me
           Bob, and I could run faster and play
           harder and do better than any boy I
           ever met! And my hair? It was all
           the way down to there! And when I
           asked my Mama - Mama? - She said, we
           have been here since the Seventeen
           Hundreds, Eloise, and in your blood
           runs the blood of Red Roberts! Do
           you know who he is? A pirate, with

flamin' red hair and a flamin' red
beard who harboured off a cove in
P.E.I.! A pirate! And inside of me —
just bustin' to get out! To reach
out! To grow!... And when I sat on
our front porch and I looked out —
I always looked up, cause lookin' up
I saw the sky, and the sky went on
forever! And I picked and sold
berries, and my Mama cleaned house
for everyone all around, and my sisters
and my one brother Bill, everything
for one thing. For me. For Eloise
Roberts. For Bob.

    (Shift. EV enters, carrying his
    bag. He is speaking to OSCAR)

EV: You know somethin'!? The goddamn
health care services in this province
are a laugh!

BOB: Katie?

EV: I had a woman come into my office
yesterday. I've never seen her before,
but she's got a lump in her breast and
she's half out of her mind with worry.
Surer than hell it's cancer, but
there's nothin' I can do till I damn
well find out it is cancer. So what
do I have to do? I gotta take a
section and ship that tissue to Saint
John on the bus for Christ's sake!
And then what? I got to wait for
three days to maybe a week to hear.
Do you know how often I get a replay
of that scenario? She's a mother or
she works for a living or she's at
home lookin' after her old man and I

can't tell her what's wrong or what
we have to do till I get that goddamn
report back from Saint John! We need
a medical laboratory in this town, and
by God, I'm gonna see that we get one!

OSCAR: Have you seen Bob?

EV: When?

OSCAR: Do you know you've a son?

EV: Georgie, we're callin' him Georgie, a
brother for Katie. Hell of a good-
lookin' boy, have you seen him?

OSCAR: I popped into the nursery.

EV: Looks like his old man.

OSCAR: Where were you?

EV: Had a call in Keswick.

OSCAR: What the hell would take you to
Keswick when your wife's in labour?

EV: I hear it went as smooth as silk.

OSCAR: Ev?

EV: ...Frank Johnston's kid fell under a
thresher.

OSCAR: Bad?

EV: Bad as it can get.

OSCAR: You...could have sent someone else.

EV: Frank's been a patient of mine since I
             started practice. Who the hell else
             could I send?

OSCAR: What about Bob?

EV: Valma was with her.

OSCAR: She didn't want Valma, she wanted you.

EV: Look, I brought Frank Johnston's kid
             into the world - and eight hours ago
             I saw him out, kneelin' in a field,
             with the kid's blood soakin' my pants.
             ...And afterwards, I sat in the kitchen
             with his mother, and before I left, I
             shared a mickey of rum with Frank.

OSCAR: It was important to Bob you be here,
             she needed you.

                  (OSCAR may exit. EV calls after
                  him)

EV: Well Frank Johnston needed me more!

                  (EV looks at CATHERINE)

             The last baby I delivered was in a
             tarpaper shack. They paid me seven
             eggs, and when the crabapples fall,
             the mother's bringin' some round.
             Would you like to talk need to that
             woman?...

                  (CATHERINE looks away)

             She's got the best maternity care this
             province provides, and the best
             obstetrician in town. She's got a

private nurse, and a baby boy. What
the hell else does she want?

(EV carries a chair over near BOB)

CATHERINE: She wants you.

EV: She's got me.

(EV sits beside BOB. Shift)

BOB: I like Robert.

EV: I thought it was George or William.

BOB: Robbie's better.

EV: What's wrong with George?

BOB: Nothing's wrong with it, I like Robbie
               best.

EV: George was my brother's name.

BOB: I know.

EV: Robert George?

BOB: Robert Dann.

EV: Where the hell did you get that name?

BOB: Out of my head.

EV: Well, you can stick George in
               someplace, can't you?

BOB: I'm not calling him George.

EV: It's my goddamn brother's name!

BOB: I know.

EV: It means a lot to my mother.

BOB: I know.

EV: So stick it in some place!

BOB: No.

EV: Jesus Christ do you have to make an issue outa every little thing?

BOB: I don't like George.

EV: What the hell harm does it do to stick George in somewhere. Robert Dann George, George Robert Dann, George Damn Robert.

BOB: He's my son.

EV: He's our son.

BOB: So register him whatever you like.

EV: I will. (stands up)

BOB: I'm calling him Robbie.

EV: (returns chair to original position) I work my ass off. Why do I do it if it's not for her?

CATHERINE: Why?

EV: For her. Oscar!

(Shift.   OSCAR may enter)

OSCAR: Ah-huh?

EV: What're your evenings like?

OSCAR: What're your evenings like?

EV: I'm doin' rounds at night and squeezin'
            in house calls after that - could you
            drop over to see her till she comes
            round a bit?

OSCAR: What about my house calls?

EV: You never made a house call in your
            life.

OSCAR: I made one once.

EV: You lazy son of a bitch. If it weren't
            for the remnants of your old man's
            practice, you'd starve to death.
            What'll you do when the last of his
            patients die off?

OSCAR: Move some place where it's hot.

EV: Listen, what she needs is someone to
            talk to, play a little golf, shit, the
            Medical Ball's comin' up next month,
            take her to that. I'm too goddman
            busy.

OSCAR: When do you sleep?

EV: I don't.

OSCAR: How the hell did she ever get pregnant?

EV: I didn't say I never laid down.

(EV may exit with bag. Shift)

BOB: I want to go to New York next month.
Go to New York and see the shows –
do you want to do that?

(Sound of Forties dance music)

OSCAR: Can Ev get away?

BOB: We'll ask.

(OSCAR lights BOB's cigarette)

Look around us. Look at all these
pursey little lips. Look at all these
doctors' wives. Do I look like that?
Do I?

OSCAR: Not a bit.

BOB: (holding glass) Well thas good.
Look at them... D'you know I joined
the I.O.D.E.? The I.O.D.E. I joined
it. And do you wanna know what's
really frightenin'? I could prolly,
after a bit, I could prolly achully –
forget. I could get to like the
I.O.D.E. Isn't tha' frightening?...
Isn't tha' frightening!... Ah, you're
as bad as Everett. Whasa matter with
doctors, you're a doctor, you tell me,
so busy savin' lives you've forgotten
how to talk? Talk!

OSCAR: The I.O.D.E. eh?

BOB: Thas right...next year I might
                run as Grand Something...The
                I.O.D.E. does some very importan'
                work you know.

                        (OSCAR smiles and casually takes
                        the glass from her)

                ...I don't like anybody here, do
                you?...

                        (BOB takes the glass back as
                        casually, takes a drink)

                Do you know my mother...and all my
                sisters...and my one brother Bill who
                taught me how to fish - hey! We
                could go fishing some time if you
                want.

OSCAR: Bob.

BOB: Everett doesn't fish! Everett doesn't
                do anything except go...round...

OSCAR: Bob.

BOB: Anyway - so all these people, mother,
                sisters, Bill, they all worked to put
                me through nursing, wasn't that
                wonderful of them?... And now Ev,
                he lent Bill the money for something
                Bill thinks he wants to do and it'll
                all be a disaster cause it's about the
                tenth time he'd done it, but Ev's
                always giving money to his mother,
                so I don't care. Why should I care?
                But you know what I don't like? Do
                you?

OSCAR: What don't you like?

BOB: I don't like the cleanin' lady.
              Because every time...the cleanin'
              lady comes in, I think of my Mama who
              cleaned all around so I could go into
              nursing

                    (Music out; silence)

              and you want to know what's worse?
              My Mama's so happy I married a doctor.
              I'm successful you see. I made
              something of myself. (moves away
              smiling; lifting her glass in a toast)
              I married a doctor.

                    (Shift. KATIE carries a hair
                    brush)

KATIE: Why don't you get married?

OSCAR: I'm waiting for you.

KATIE: I'm not related to you.

OSCAR: No.

KATIE: But you're always here, you're always
              about... Do you love my mother?

OSCAR: I love you.

KATIE: Do you want to brush my hair?

OSCAR: If you want me to.

KATIE: You can if you want.

                  (KATIE gives OSCAR the brush, and
                  sits at his feet. He brushes
                  her hair. She enjoys it for a
                  moment before speaking)

                  I'm named after my Gramma, but I'm not
like my Gramma. ...I know when trains
are coming...and when they're coming,
I don't go that way then... Do you
like brushing my hair?

OSCAR: It needs it.

KATIE: I don't care if it's messy. It's how
you are inside that counts.

OSCAR: That's true.

KATIE: I'm surprised you don't know that.

CATHERINE: Did you love my mother, Uncle Oscar?

OSCAR: When your mother's not well, you
should think about that.

KATIE: About what?

OSCAR: How she feels inside.

KATIE: ...I wonder - what my father sees in
you. (grabs the hairbrush) You're
not a very good doctor. What does he
see in you?

OSCAR: Katie -

KATIE: Do you like brushing my hair?
Do you like brushing my hair!

OSCAR: Katie -

KATIE: I hate you!

> (KATIE moves away from OSCAR, who follows her. Shift. BOB moves to the liquor and refills her glass. It is late, and she drinks while she waits)

BOB: Ev!...is that you, Ev?

> (EV may enter. He will sit, his bag at his feet, with his head back and his eyes closed)

EV: Yeah.

BOB: What time is it? ...Where were you?

EV: Just left the hospital. They brought in some kid with a ruptured spleen... car accident...took out every guard rail on that big turn on River Road ...damn near bled out when we got him.

BOB: How is he?

EV: Mnn?

BOB: I said, how is he?

EV: Bout half a million pieces...

BOB: ...Ev?

EV: What time is it?

BOB: Late.

EV: Takin' out a stomach in the mornin'.

BOB: ...Can we talk?

EV: Talk away...

BOB: I let the maid go today. It wasn't
             working out -

EV: Medjuck call?

BOB: What?

EV: Did Sam Medjuck call?

BOB: I said I let the maid go today -

EV: Mn?

BOB: (moves to refill her drink) Valma
             phoned and said he'd called her.

EV: Christ. (gets up; picks up his bag)

CATHERINE: Why would he phone Valma's looking for
             you?

EV: He knows her, she kids him along.

CATHERINE: Were you over at Valma's?

EV: I was takin' out a spleen.

CATHERINE: Should I believe that?

EV: I was takin' out a spleen!

BOB: I said I let the maid go today!

EV: How many's that?

BOB: She was a smarmy bitch and I fired her!

EV: I said how many's that?

               (EV may exit)

BOB: Where're you going?

EV: (offstage) House call to Medjuck's!

BOB: It's the middle of the night!

EV: (offstage) It's morning!

BOB: Ev! Ev!

CATHERINE: He's gone.

BOB: You'll fall asleep, Ev! You'll fall
               asleep and run off the road!

KATIE: Shut up Mummy!

BOB: Ev!

KATIE: Why don't you shut up and let people
               sleep!

BOB: Oscar!

CATHERINE: He isn't here, Mummy!

BOB: Count on Oscar!

KATIE: He's not here, Mummy!

OSCAR: When you need me you call, I'll be
               there.

CATHERINE: Daddy!

               (EV may enter, isolated on stage.
               Music filters in, "Auld Lang Syne")

EV: Buy a Packard I always say! Best goddamn car on the road!

CATHERINE: Do something.

EV: I'd be drivin' along, middle of the night -

BOB: It's seven maids, that's how many!

EV: All of a sudden, swish, swish, swish, tree branches hittin' the car, look around -

BOB: And I'll fire the next seven whenever I damn well feel like it!

CATHERINE: Daddy!

EV: Car's in the middle of a goddamn orchard.

BOB: Oscar!

EV: I've fallen asleep and failed to navigate a turn and here's me and the car travellin' through this goddamn orchard.

> (BOB is joined by OSCAR. They
> dance to "Auld Lang Syne", as
> KATIE watches. CATHERINE's
> focus slowly switches, from her
> father to BOB and OSCAR)

BOB: Oscar.

EV: And me without a clue in the world as to where I'm headed. Black as pitch, not a light to be seen, and me drivin' over bumps and skirtin' fences and tryin' to remember where in the hell I'm goin'. Then I catch a glimpse of this little light, almost like a low-lyin' star in the sky.

(BOB kisses OSCAR)

EV: ...head for that - what the hell - could end up on Venus! Door opens and someone is standin' there--

(BOB sees KATIE watching)

"We been waitin' for you, Doc."

BOB: What do you want?

EV: "Is the coffee hot?"

BOB: What do you want!

EV: "Melt a spoon."

KATIE: (screams) Don't! You don't!

(KATIE launches herself at OSCAR and BOB)

EV: "We been waitin' for you, Doc."

(KATIE hits OSCAR and BOB and BOB steps away from OSCAR. During all the action she continues to scream)

KATIE: You! You! Get away! Get away! I hate you! I hate you! You don't! Get away!

(Catherine runs to KATIE and
tries to restrain her)

CATHERINE: Stop. Stop. Daddy. Daddy!!

(KATIE collapses against CATHERINE)

Help me.

End of Act One

Act Two

> The house is silent. EV and
> CATHERINE are most prominent
> on stage. KATIE is not far
> from CATHERINE. BOB and OSCAR
> are in the background.
> CATHERINE looks at EV, who is
> wearing an old cardigan and
> glasses. CATHERINE holds
> Gramma's letter.

CATHERINE: ...Go on.

EV: ...When I was little, Katie...when I
was a kid, I saw my own father get
smaller and smaller, physically
smaller, cause he was nothin', no job,
no...nothin'. I was only a kid but I
saw him...get smaller like that...
Georgie now, he was the one in our
family would have gone places.

CATHERINE: Haven't you "gone places"?

EV: Seen half this province from their
mother's belly to the grave.

CATHERINE: Was it worth it?

EV: ...When that goddamn Demsky let me up,
I'd wander all round the hospital.
I'd look in the wards, Intensive Care
...You get to be my age, the only
place better than a hospital for
meetin' people you know is a mortuary
...Frank Johnston died while I was
there in his room. They had him
hooked up to all these goddamn
monitors. And do you know how they
knew he was dead? Straight lines and
the sound from the monitors. Nobody
looked down at Frank. Just at the
monitors... And that is the kinda
hospital they're gonna put my name on?
...I wouldn't like to go like Frank.

CATHERINE: You won't go for ages, Daddy.

EV: If I can keep away from that Demsky
I got a chance...

CATHERINE: Daddy?

EV: What?

CATHERINE: About Mummy.

EV: ...If I could - I'm gonna show you
somethin', I want you to see this...
you see this, you'll understand.
(opens trunk and begins to sort
through it) Six or seven kids standin'
by the car, and the car outsida this
Day Clinic... Valma and I, we were doin
these check-ups and physicals and what-
have-you...where the hell...we were doin

that one day a week in Minto, families
a miners, poor goddamn buggers, most
of 'em unemployed at the time. And
this bunch a little rag-tag snotty-
nosed kids, smellin' a wet wool and
Javex, were impressed all to hell by
the car - and Valma, out with the
goddamn camera, and she took this here
picture...it's in here, where the hell
is it? (stops looking for the snapshot)
...I don't care about this hospital
thing, I don't care about... I cared
about those little kids! I looked
into their faces, and I saw my own
face when I was a kid...was I wrong to
do that? So goddamn much misery -
should I have tended my own little
plot when I looked round and there
was so damn much to do - so much I
could do - I did do! Goddamn it, I
did it! You tell me, was I wrong to
do that!

> (Pause. EV is about to look again
> for the picture)

CATHERINE: It isn't there, Daddy.

EV: I had to rely on myself cause there
             was fuckin' little else to rely on, I
             made decisions when decisions had to
             be made, I chose a road, and I took
             it, and I never looked back.

CATHERINE: You've always been so sure of things,
             haven't you.

> (EV watches CATHERINE as she looks
> down at the envelope, and turns
> it over in her hands)

82

EV: ...You're like her, Katie.

CATHERINE: Like Gramma?

EV: Like your mother. (removes his
             glasses)

CATHERINE: She always said I was just like you.

EV: Like her.

CATHERINE: Don't say that.

KATIE: Am I like Gramma, Daddy?

EV: You're like yourself, Katie.

KATIE: Why don't you open it, Daddy?

             (KATIE is looking at the letter
              CATHERINE holds)

EV: I will.

CATHERINE: When I was little I stayed with her
             once.

             (CATHERINE looks at KATIE)

EV: After your mother had Robbie.

KATIE: And I swore, and she said, "You never
             say those words, Katie, only in
             church," and when I dropped my prayer
             book I said, "Jesus Christ, Gramma"
             and she said, "Ka-Ty!"

CATHERINE: And I said, "But we are in church,
             Gramma."

(KATIE and CATHERINE laugh. EV
takes off the old cardigan and
hangs it over his chair as he
speaks)

EV: She'd write that kinda thing in a
letter. That's all that she'd write.
That's what's in that letter. (exits)

CATHERINE: (to KATIE) I don't want to be like
her, and I don't want to be like
Mummy.

KATIE: (sings to CATHERINE)
K-K-K-Katie, my beautiful Katie,
You the only G-G-G-Girl that I adore
When the M-M-M-Moon shines

(KATIE looks at a note book; she
has not carried one before)

I'll be waiting...
K-K-K-Katie...Katie...

(Shift. OSCAR is watching KATIE)

(to CATHERINE) Everything's down in here.
I write it all down. And when I grow
up, I'll have it all here.

CATHERINE: Will it be worth it?

KATIE: I used to pray to God, but I don't
anymore. I write it all down in here.
I was just little then and now -

(KATIE senses OSCAR is watching
her)

Are you interested in this, Uncle Oscar?
Cause if you aren't, why do you listen?

OSCAR: For you.

KATIE: I don't like people doing things for
           me. I can do things for myself...

                    (KATIE starts to write in the
                    book, the only time she does so)

           "Now Mummy has a 'medical problem'
           p-r-ob." Did you know that, Uncle
           Oscar? Mummy has a <u>medical problem</u> -
           that's apart from her <u>personal</u>
           <u>problems</u>, did you know that?

OSCAR: No.

KATIE: Really?

                    (Shift. EV enters with bag and
                    suit jacket. OSCAR may help him
                    on with it)

EV: I thought you knew.

OSCAR: How the hell would I know?

EV: I'm sending her to the Royal Vic.

OSCAR: Who to?

EV: You remember Bob Greene from McGill?

OSCAR: Bit quick to cut, isn't he?

EV: You never liked him.

OSCAR: Neither did you.

EV: So he's an asshole, was, is, and will
           be, but he's goddamn good at his job.

OSCAR: He's too quick to cut.

EV: And the best gynecologist in the country.

OSCAR: He'll have her in surgery before the ink on her train ticket dries.

EV: This is your professional opinion, is it, based on your _extensive_ practice?

OSCAR: There's gotta be other options.

EV: We could go someplace where it's hot and lie in the sun till she grows a tumor the size of a melon - why don't we do that?

OSCAR: I -

EV: You wanna look at her medical records? Go talk to Barney, tell him I said to pull 'em and show you - fibrous uterus, two opinions.

OSCAR: Greene'll go for radical surgery and -

EV: What the hell do you want me to do?

OSCAR: Does she know?

EV: Of course she knows! What the hell do you mean, does she know?

OSCAR: You gotta take some time with her, she's gonna need that.

EV: I got no time.

OSCAR: What's wrong with just takin' off - the two of you go just as soon as she's able.

EV: I can't.

OSCAR: Look, you lie on the sand in the sun
           and you relax for Christ's sake.

EV: I got patients been waitin' for a bed
           for months, I can't just leave 'em to
           whoever's on call.

OSCAR: I'll take 'em, you go.

EV: They count on me bein' there, Oscar.

OSCAR: The population of this province will
           not wither and die if you take a three
           week vacation - I'll handle your
           patients.

EV: I'd go nuts doin' nothin'.

OSCAR: You're doin' it for her.

EV: I'd go nuts.

OSCAR: You're drivin' her nuts!

EV: Were that to be true, three weeks in
           the sun wouldn't change it.

OSCAR: Don't think of her as your wife -
           think of her as a patient who's married
           to an insensitive son-of-a-bitch.

EV: I was an insensitive son-of-a-bitch
           when she met me; I haven't changed.

OSCAR: I give up.

EV: O.K. O.K., I'm thinking...I'm
           thinking... I'm thinking you like
           sand and sun, you could take her.

OSCAR: I didn't marry her.

EV: You like her.

OSCAR: I like her.

EV: She likes you.

OSCAR: Listen to yourself! You're asking me
           to take your wife on a three week
           vacation to recover from major surgery,
           do you realize that?

EV: She needs to get away, I can't take
           the time, you can.

OSCAR: It's one thing I'm not gonna do for
           you.

EV: So do it for her.

OSCAR: No.

EV: It makes sense to me.

OSCAR: No.

EV: Why not?

OSCAR: No, I said no.

EV: You're the one suggested it.

OSCAR: I didn't.

                    (EV looks at his watch)

           We're not leaving it there!

EV: Look. There's an alumnae thing in
         six or seven months, I can schedule
         around it and the three of us'll have
         one hell of a good bash, but right
         now I cannot get away so I'm askin'
         you to do me this favour. How often
         do I ask for a favour? Take her to
         one of those islands you go to, eat
         at the clubs, lie in the sun, and -
         Christ, Oscar, I got to go, so gimme
         an answer, yes or no? (pause) You
         make the arrangements, I'll pick up
         the tab.

OSCAR: Half the tab.

EV: Fifty-fifty all the way.

OSCAR: Are you sure you don't want me to
         check her into the Vic, observe the
         surgery, hang around the recovery
         room and generally be there?

EV: I can clear three or four days for
         that.

              (OSCAR is silent. As EV is about
               to leave he notices OSCAR's
               silence and stops)

         Say - how did that burn case go?

OSCAR: That was four months ago, Ev.

EV: Seems like yesterday, so how did it go?

OSCAR: Zip, kaput.

EV: What the hell did you do?

OSCAR: Did it ever occur to you that I might find Bob very attractive?

EV: I know she's attractive, hell, I married her, didn't I?

OSCAR: That she might find me very attractive?

EV: Don't let it go to your head.

OSCAR: You know rumours fly.

EV: I'm too damned busy to listen to rumours.

OSCAR: Your mother isn't. She listens. After that, she phones.

EV: Who?

OSCAR: Me. She phones me. To talk about you. She's a remnant of my old man's practice, remember?

EV: Last time I saw her she didn't -

OSCAR: When was that anyway?

EV: Oh I was over - no - ah -

OSCAR: She can't remember either. I've seen you, you son-of-a-bitch, I've seen you take time with some old biddy, you laugh, you hang onto her hand, and she leaves your office thinking she's Claudette Colbert, and has just stolen a night with you at the Ritz - and I - I get the phone calls from your mother who is reduced to writing you letters and crying to me on the

phone. You don't call, you don't
visit, you don't...and now she's
got it into her head that...

EV: What?

OSCAR: Rumours fly.

EV: So you reassure her. I gotta go,
             Oscar.

OSCAR: What if I can't reassure her?

EV: Then you laugh, hang onto her hand,
             and make Mum think she's Claudette
             Colbert at the Ritz.

OSCAR: It's not that simple.

                 (EV is moving away from OSCAR)

             I do find Bob very attractive!

EV: Total agreement.

OSCAR: You never think for one minute there
             could be one iota of truth in those
             rumours?

EV: I just don't believe you'd do that to
             me.

OSCAR: How can you be so sure?

EV: I know you.

OSCAR: Better than I know myself?

EV: I must. (speaking as he exits)
             Barbados eh, or someplace like that.

(Shift)

BOB: I don't plan on having any more
                children.

CATHERINE: No more children.

BOB: I didn't plan, didn't.

CATHERINE: No children.

BOB: Don't have to plan now. All taken
                care of. Are you listenin' to me?

                (Shift. KATIE and CATHERINE will
                   end up together, a mirror image)

KATIE: I'll tell you what she does. What
                she does is, she starts doing
                something. Something big. That's
                how I can tell. She's all right for
                awhile - and then she decides she's
                gonna paint all of the downstairs -
                or we're gonna put in new cupboards
                - or knock out a wall!... We got
                so many walls knocked out, the house
                started to fall down in the middle!
                Can you believe that? - And we had to
                get a big steel beam put through in
                the basement! Can you believe that?

CATHERINE: It's true.

KATIE: And before she gets finished one of
                those big jobs - she starts.

CATHERINE: And she never finishes. Someone else
                comes in, and they finish.

KATIE: But that's how I can tell when she's
                gonna start. And I try to figure out

CATHERINE: I ask myself

KATIE: Does the big job make her start - or does she start the big job because she knows she's gonna start?

CATHERINE: But that's how I could tell, that's the beginning.

(Shift)

BOB: So...why does it...why do I feel that it matters? Two were enough, Katie and Robbie, so why do I feel that it matters? I don't want any more... Oscar!

OSCAR: I'm here.

BOB: Does it matter?

OSCAR: Well...from the medical -

BOB: Medical, medical, medical, I don't wanna talk about medical.

OSCAR: It affects -

BOB: Me! Me! I'm talkin' about me! Why do I feel like, why do I feel - we didn't want any more children! I can't have any more children! Me, the part of me that's important, here, inside here - Me! That's the same. I'm the same. So...why do I feel that it matters?

OSCAR: It doesn't matter.

BOB: Why don't you listen? I'm trying to
            explain. We didn't want any more, I
            can't have any more, so why does it
            matter?

OSCAR: It doesn't matter.

BOB: It does matter!... I'm the same.
            Inside I'm the same. I'm Eloise
            Roberts and they called me Bob and I
            can run faster and do better than any
            boy I ever met!

OSCAR: It's all right.

BOB: No.

OSCAR: Come here.

BOB: I try to figure it out and I just keep
            going round.

CATHERINE: It's all right.

BOB: I need to do more, I need to... I
            need...

CATHERINE: Why don't you just do what you want?

BOB: Sometimes I want to scream. I just
            want to stand there and scream, to
            hit something, to reach out and smash
            things — and hit and smash and hit
            and smash and...and then... I would
            feel very tired and I could lie down
            and sleep.

OSCAR: Do you want to sleep now?

BOB: No. I'm not tired now. I want a
            drink now. Want a drink, and then
            we'll...what will we do?

CATHERINE: Why couldn't you leave.

BOB: Leave?

CATHERINE: Just leave!

BOB: Katie and Robbie.

CATHERINE: Did you care about them?

BOB: And your father?

            (Shift. EV enters, carrying a
             bag. He is isolated on stage)

EV: We had the worst goddamn polio epidemic
            this province has seen, eleven years
            ago. We had an outbreak this year.
            You are lookin' at the attendin'
            physician at the present Polio Clinic
            - it is a building that has been
            condemned by the Provincial Fire
            Marshall, it has been condemned by the
            Provincial Health Officer, it has
            been condemned by the Victoria Public
            Hospital, it's infested by cockroaches,
            it's overrun by rats, it's the worst
            goddamn public building in this
            province! When is the government
            gonna stop building liquor stores and
            give the doctors of this province a
            chance to save a few fuckin' lives!

BOB: Haven't you got enough?

EV: Enough what?

BOB: Enough! Enough everything!

EV: You're drunk.

BOB: You'll never get enough, will you?

EV: Did Valma phone?

BOB: I don't answer the phone, just let it ring and ring –

                (EV starts to exit)

           Where're you going?

EV: Valma's.

BOB: What for?

EV: To pick up the messages that she'd give me by phone if you'd answer the phone.

BOB: Maid could answer it. Does answer it, but she's not good with messages, no.

EV: You run them through the house so goddamn fast they don't have time to pick up a phone. Why don't you get one and keep one?

BOB: Interviewin' them gives me somethin' to do. I enjoy interviewin' them. Purpose and direction to my life! Where're you goin'?

EV: (exiting) Valma's.

BOB: Stay.

CATHERINE: Stay.

             (EV stops)

          Don't go.

          Sit for a little while.

             (There is a moment of silence)

CATHERINE: Talk.

EV: If I sit down...my head will start to nod.

CATHERINE: That'd be all right. She wouldn't mind. You'd be here.

                 (EV puts down his bag. He moves to BOB and sits beside her. He takes his hat off and takes her hand. BOB smiles and strokes EV's hand, then holds it against her face)

BOB: Do you remember...sometimes I...we had some good times, didn't we?

EV: We can still have good times.

BOB: I don't know.

EV: You've got to get hold of things.

BOB: I try.

EV: I know I'm busy.

BOB: Always busy.

EV: I know.

BOB: If I could do something.

EV: There's the house and the kids. Just
           tell me what you want and I'll get it.

BOB: I can't do anything.

EV: You can.

BOB: No. There's nothing I can do.

EV: Sure there is.

                (BOB slowly shakes her head)

           Come on...hey, listen, did you know
           the Hendersons were sellin' their camp
           on the Miramichi?

                (Pause)

           Well they are. What say we buy it?
           You'd like that, wouldn't you? You
           could get away from the kids and the
           house, do some fishin', you like
           fishin' don't you?

                (BOB nods her head)

           Well, that's what we'll do. (checks
           his watch) Shit. You get to bed.
           Get some sleep. (exits)

BOB: Can't sleep.

(There is the sound of a train whistle; BOB listens to it. It fades away. Shift)

...Half-way across three-quarters of a mile of single track...its whistle would split the night, and that night ...do you know what she did?

CATHERINE: No, and neither do you.

BOB: She walked out to meet it.

CATHERINE: And you say I'm like his side of the family, you say I'm like her?

BOB: She did.

CATHERINE: I would never do that!

(Shift)

KATIE: Mummy didn't like her. I could have gone to see her with Daddy, but Daddy was always too busy to go, so it was all his fault I didn't see her... I guess that's true.

CATHERINE: She would phone, she would ask for me.

KATIE: But I could never think of anything to say... They're the ones I'm supposed to like, his side of the family, so it would have been nice to see her... was she old?...

(CATHERINE doesn't answer)

KATIE: Is that what she died of?...

            (CATHERINE doesn't answer)

            What did she die of, Uncle Oscar?

OSCAR: It was an accident.

CATHERINE: We know "accidents", don't we.

KATIE: I never saw anybody dead before. I
            don't know if I wanted to see her
            dead...it didn't matter because they
            didn't take us anyway - I was a bit
            happy not to go because I don't like
            to go anywhere with Mummy when she's
            like that. She said Gramma was a
            bitch who went around saying bad things
            about her and Mummy was glad she was
            dead - and Daddy just kept getting
            dressed and pretended Mummy wasn't
            talking - You can only pretend for
            so long.

CATHERINE: And when they came home he went out.

KATIE: And Mummy phoned all over but he
            wasn't any place she could find, and...

CATHERINE: ...then she tripped at the top of the
            stairs and she fell. I went to my
            bedroom as soon as that happened...

KATIE: ...and Robbie screamed and cried and
            screamed and cried and...

CATHERINE: ...the maid got up and put her to
            bed - she'll be leaving soon and
            we'll get a new one...

KATIE: ...you'd think if a person kept
            falling down stairs it would hurt
            them!

CATHERINE: It never did a thing to her.

            (Shift)

BOB: Katie!...Katie! You wanna know
            somethin'?

KATIE: No.

BOB: Your father's mother killed herself!...

            (Pause. KATIE stares at BOB)

            You look at me...you look at me and
            what are you thinking?

KATIE: Nothing.

BOB: This isn't me you know. This isn't
            really me. This is someone else...
            What are you thinking?

KATIE: I don't think anything.

BOB: Katie!

CATHERINE: Leave her alone.

BOB: You know what your father's mother
            said?

CATHERINE: Leave her alone!

BOB: Do you know?

KATIE: No!

BOB: Why would a nurse - to catch a doctor, that's why. Why would he marry me, eh? Why would a brilliant young man, whole life ahead of him, why would he marry me? Eh? Do you know why? Do you know!

KATIE: No.

BOB: Why would he do that?!

KATIE: I don't know.

BOB: Answer me!

KATIE: I don't know!

BOB: No! You don't know! Nobody knows!

KATIE: I know. Inside I know. He had to.

CATHERINE: Don't.

KATIE: Inside I do know. Because of me - and that's what went wrong.

CATHERINE: He loved her and she loved him, Uncle Oscar says.

KATIE: No.

CATHERINE: That's true, Katie!

KATIE: Do you believe that?

(EV enters in his shirt sleeves)

Daddy!

                    (KATIE runs to EV and he puts
                    his arms around her)

EV: Your mother sometimes says things that
            she doesn't mean. She's sick and she –

KATIE: She isn't sick!

EV: She loves you.

KATIE: I don't love her.

                    (KATIE quickly moves away. EV
                    starts after her)

EV: Yes you do.

                    (Shift)

BOB: Valma, Valma, Valma, Valma, Valma,
            Valma I am so sick of that woman's
            name. What're you and her doing,
            that's what I'd like to know!

EV: Nothing. (sits)

BOB: Oooh, you don't tell me that! I know
            better than that! She's like your
            right arm, your left arm, part of your
            leg!

EV: Leave Valma out of it.

BOB: I don't wanna leave Valma out of it!
            She'd do anything for you – put your
            wife to bed, get her up – why does
            she do that, eh? Tell me why?

EV: She's the best office nurse in the
            city and I couldn't run that office
            without her. Why the Christ don't you
            go to bed?

BOB: Why the Christ don't you go to bed?

EV: Go to bed.

BOB: Gonna go over to Valma's and go to bed? You don't love me, you never loved me! You never loved me.

EV: Go to bed.

BOB: You don't even see me. You look at me and there's nobody there. You don't see anybody but those stupid stupid people who think you're God. You're not God!

                (CATHERINE and KATIE are together and BOB moves towards them. BOB grabs CATHERINE's hand)

        And it's so funny...do you know what he's done, do you know?... If I... If I go into the liquor store, do you know what happens? They say...sorry, but the Doc says <u>no</u>. He says...they're not to...and they don't. They don't. He tells them don't sell it to her the Doc says don't do that and they don't. But what's so funny is...every drunk in the city goes into that office on Saturday and they say... "Jeez Chris Doc, spend the whole cheque on booze, the old lady's gonna kill me," and he gives them money... Gives <u>them</u> money.

                (KATIE moves away)

        And Valma says he says maybe one of them takes it home instead of just buyin' more, can you believe that?...

104

And when I go in, they say, "The Doc
says no" ...but I don't have to worry.
(moves to refill her glass) so long
as I keep interviewin' the maids...
I don't have to worry about a thing.

(Shift)

KATIE: You don't have any family.

OSCAR: You're my family.

KATIE: I'm not related to you, and you're not
related to me, you can't be family,
Uncle Oscar.

(Shift)

BOB: (leaves her glass) Hey! Do you
want to know what a bastard he is?

(CATHERINE turns her head away as
BOB advances on EV)

Well I don't care if you want to know
or not - I'm gonna tell you. I put
the clothes out, put the suit out for
the cleaners and I went through his
pockets, and do you know what I found,
do you know? It was something he
didn't need for me, something he
wouldn't use with me, because I can't
have any more, no, I've been fixed
like the goddamn cat or the dog so
what the hell did you have it for?

EV: If you found it, that means I didn't
use it, so what the hell's your
problem?

(BOB runs at EV)

BOB: You bastard!

(BOB strikes at EV's chest. He grabs her wrists)

You bastard you.

(BOB attempts to strike EV several times before collapsing against EV's chest. He picks her up, carries her to a chair and puts her in it. He looks down at her for a moment, then moves away, to sit isolated on the stage. OSCAR joins him. Shift)

OSCAR: She tells me you're bangin' Valma.

EV: If I wanted to bang someone, it sure as hell wouldn't be Valma.

OSCAR: So who are you bangin'?

EV: Has she posted that condom story in the staff room, or is it just you she's told?

OSCAR: I asked you a question.

EV: I'm not bangin' anyone! Who the hell are you bangin'!... I...I lost Jack Robinson the other night... I felt so goddamn bad. I thought he was gonna make it and then everything started shuttin' down. He gets pneumonia, we get that under control, then his heart starts givin' us

106

problems, we get that solved, then
his goddamn kidneys go - I don't
know why, just one thing after another.
Someone was callin' his name and I
couldn't do a damn thing about it...
and I felt so bad, I thought...I don't
want to go home, you can see what
she's like so...you know what I did?
I bought a mickey of rum and that
goddamn condom and I...I drove around
for a coupla hours. And that was it...
That was it.

OSCAR: Things can't go on.

EV: Don't start on that give her more time
           shit. Her problem's got nothin' to
           do with time nor work nor any other
           goddamn thing.

OSCAR: Her problem is the crazy son-of-a-bitch
           she's married to.

EV: Who the hell is crazy here? I'm the
           one can't keep a bottle of booze in
           the house, I'm the one's gotta put the
           fear of God in the help so they're too
           damn scared to buy it for her - and
           now she's into the vanilla or any other
           goddamn thing she can pour down her
           throat! I can't keep pills in the bag
           and she'd let the kids starve to death
           if it weren't for the maid! I'm the
           one goin' eighteen hours a day tryin'
           to hold the fuckin' fort so I can hear
           you say what!? That I'm crazy! I'm
           not a goddamn machine!!! I thought if
           anyone would understand, it would be
           you...and you... (exits)

OSCAR: Ev. Ev!

            (OSCAR may exit after him. Shift.
            BOB runs her hand along the
            cushion in the chair. She gets
            on her knees, lifts the cushion
            up. CATHERINE watches her search.
            KATIE too observes, from a
            distance. BOB continues her
            search)

BOB: Everyone has something hidden in this
            house. I hide it and he hides it and
            you hide it.

CATHERINE: Do something.

BOB: Do something. Just like your father.
            Do, do, do.

CATHERINE: Just stop!

BOB: Just stop. (finds bottle of pills)
            Stop doing. (unscrews bottle; pours
            pills in hand; looks at CATHERINE)
            Stop. (swallows pills; settles back
            in chair; shuts eyes)

            (Shift. KATIE slowly approaches
            BOB. She and CATHERINE stand,
            looking at BOB. Pause)

KATIE: She was blue... I'd never seen anybody
            blue before. Robbie went in the
            kitchen and cried. I stood at the
            bottom of the stairs and watched them
            bring her down on the stretcher. I
            didn't cry... I don't know what she
            took - was it the pills that make
            her sleep?

108

CATHERINE: Uncle Oscar said.

KATIE: She was asleep all right. And really
              blue. I thought... I thought...

CATHERINE: Go on, you can say it.

KATIE: I thought maybe she was dead. (moves
              away) ...and now she's going to
              Connecticut? Will she be better then?

              (CATHERINE joins KATIE)

CATHERINE: Uncle Oscar said.

KATIE: All better?

              (CATHERINE doesn't answer)

              I wonder...do you know what I wonder?
              I wonder, did she take the pills to
              sleep like she sometimes does, or did
              she...

CATHERINE: It was

KATIE: An accident?... Sometimes I look...

CATHERINE: ...in the mirror, I look in the
              mirror...

KATIE: ...and I see Mummy and I see...

CATHERINE: ...Gramma, and Mummy and me...

KATIE: ...I don't want to be like them.

              (Shift. OSCAR may enter. BOB is
              sitting. She will get up and
              very carefully tie her gown.

> There is a certain formality,
> seriousness, alienation and
> deliberation about her. She
> moves and speaks somewhat slowly.
> OSCAR stands a distance from
> her, still and watching)

BOB: You have to get hold of things.
Routine's important. Get out. Get
around. Do things. The I.O.D.E.,
Bridge... The doctors' wives have
this sort of club and it meets on a
regular basis, I...

OSCAR: Tired?

BOB: No. Feeling fine. How do I look?

OSCAR: Good.

> (BOB moves to another chair and
> sits. OSCAR remains in the same
> position, watching her. BOB
> doesn't speak till seated. She
> does not look at OSCAR)

BOB: Leisure activity is big. Structured
leisure activity. Very big. (pause)
Painting. I paint now. You know.
(pause) Pictures. (pause; speaks
softly) What else? (pause) Gorgeous
place. If you'd been there, it would
have been perfect. (pause; speaks
softly) What else. (pause)
Psychiatrists, psychiatrists. They
ask you obvious things and you give
them obvious answers. It's all very
obvious... Obvious... (softly)
what else. (long pause; softly)
Nothing...nothing else...I can't think
of...anything else.

                    (BOB sits very still. OSCAR
                    stands watching her. BOB begins
                    to rock back and forth very
                    slightly and sings very softly
                    to herself. She is not singing
                    words, but merely making sounds.
                    OSCAR moves to her. He stands
                    behind her looking down for a
                    moment. He slowly places a hand
                    on her shoulder. She reaches up
                    and holds his hand pressing it
                    to her shoulder. She continues
                    to rock slightly but the words
                    of the song can be heard. She is
                    singing "Auld Lang Syne". OSCAR
                    moves around her without letting
                    go of her hand and draws her up
                    to dance, which they do rather
                    formally)

BOB: (sings) Should auld acquaintance be
                    forgot
                and never brought to mind
                Should auld acquaintance
                Be forgot - and auld lang syne
                an auld lang syne m'dear
                an auld lang syne

                    (BOB begins to cry but continues
                    singing and dancing)

                Let's drink a cup of kindness up
                For auld lang syne

                    (Shift. EV enters. He is
                    isolated on stage. He carries
                    his bag, and his hat is pushed
                    back on his head. There is an
                    air of powerful relaxation and
                    poise about him. He might almost

(be standing in a glow of golden
sunshine. When he speaks BOB and
OSCAR stop dancing. They turn to
stare at him and OSCAR will step
away from BOB. BOB is drawn
towards EV, who does not
acknowledge her)

EV: I say three or four of us go in
together. I mean look at the situation
now. A patient comes in from Durham
Bridge, and has to run all over this
Christless city, G.P. here, lab tests
there, pediatrician someplace else.
I've got my eye on a place on the
hill. We renovate it -

BOB: Bar date with him.

EV: And we open a Medical Clinic, lab,
X-ray, everything in that one
building -

BOB: And you don't call that -

EV: We solicit the best specialists we can
to take office space there. We give
the people of this goddamn province
the medical care they deserve, without
havin' to run all over hell and hackety
to get it!

BOB: And I laughed - and he said - and
it was so funny - such a long time
ago...

        (Shift)

KATIE: You lied to me.

OSCAR: When?

KATIE: People lie to me quite a bit. They
            think I don't know it, but I do.

OSCAR: I didn't mean to lie.

KATIE: You didn't tell the truth.

OSCAR: What did I lie about?

KATIE: Guess - one guess.

BOB: S'funny thing.

KATIE: You promised me she'd get better,
            Uncle Oscar! You promised and you
            lied!

                (Shift. BOB lights a cigarette
                during her speech. By the end
                of her speech it is apparent
                she's been drinking)

BOB: The more you do of certain things,
             the less it seems you do. You fill
             your time up, my time's filled up.
             I sit at these tea luncheons, s'always
             ...sherry. I hate sherry. I never
             have any sherry. I know what they
             think, but that's not the reason. I
             just don't like sherry. No. No
             sherry. (pause) Children are
             important. (pause) And the I.O.D.E.
             ...I go to - and bridshe, play a lot
             of bridshe, I'm good at that. Win,
             always win. ...I like bridshe. And
             ahh (pause) I don't really like them
             but - everything's working for them
             and everything can work for me too.

I can be them. It isn't hard, I can
do it. I can. If I...if I want to.

> (BOB moves to drawer, opens it
> and feels inside. She is looking
> for a bottle, slowly and
> methodically. She becomes aware
> of KATIE watching her)

BOB: What do you want?

KATIE: I don't want anything.

BOB: What're you doing?

KATIE: I'm watching you.

BOB: Your father tell you to do that?

KATIE: No.

BOB: Then why are you watchin'?

KATIE: I want to remember.

BOB: Remember what?

KATIE: Remember you.

BOB: I know what you're thinking. It's
            all right. You can say it...do you
            want me to say it?

KATIE: No.

BOB: I'm not afraid. I can say it.

KATIE: If I were you - I wouldn't let Robbie
            see me like that. It makes him feel
            bad. He has to pretend that you're
            sick.

BOB: What do you pretend, Katie?

KATIE: I don't have to pretend anymore.

CATHERINE: Katie.

            (BOB stops her search, turns to
            KATIE)

BOB: Did you take something of mine?

KATIE: Did I?

BOB: You took something of mine and I want
            it back.

KATIE: You can't have it back.

BOB: I want it back!

KATIE: It's gone.

BOB: No.

KATIE: I poured it out, let go!

BOB: Give it back!

CATHERINE: Don't.

            (BOB and KATIE struggle)

BOB: You had no right you...

KATIE: Let go!

BOB: No.

CATHERINE: Let her go.

BOB: Give it to me.

KATIE: Let go, let go!

BOB: You you no right!

KATIE: Go!

            (KATIE strikes at BOB, knocking
            her down)

            I'm not gonna cry. I'm not gonna cry!

BOB: I tried. I really did try.

CATHERINE: I'm not gonna cry.

BOB: Listen.

            (BOB grabs CATHERINE's hand)

            Listen Katie. I want... I want to
            tell you - when - when I was little,
            do you know, do you know I would sit
            on our front porch, and I would look
            up, look up at the sky, and the sky,
            the sky went on forever. And I just
            looked up. That was me, Katie.
            That was me.

CATHERINE: I'm holding my breath and my teeth
            are together and my tongue, I can feel
            my tongue, it presses hard on the back
            of my teeth and the roof of my mouth...

KATIE: ...and I hang on really tight. Really
            tight, and then...I don't cry.

CATHERINE: I never cried...(to BOB) but I
            couldn't listen like that.

116

                    (BOB releases CATHERINE's hands,
                    and moves away from her.
                    CATHERINE runs after her as she
                    speaks)

CATHERINE: It's one of the things you can't do
             like that!

KATIE: It's better not to cry than to listen.

CATHERINE: Is it?

KATIE: It's how you keep on. It's one of the
             ways. I'm surprised you don't know
             that.

                    (KATIE moves away from CATHERINE,
                    who then follows her. Shift)

EV: Close this time.

OSCAR: How close?

EV: Too damn close. We pumped her stomach
             and prayed. The kids spent Christmas
             Day at Valma's... I think... I think
             the psychiatrist she sees is nuttier
             than she is. ...I'm alright...

                    (EV sits in the same chair he sat
                    in as "Old Ev", at the start of
                    the play. Pause)

             Did you know...what the hell is their
             name...live over on King Street,
             married someone or other, moved to
             Toronto... I'm alright.   (pause)
             Some silly son of a whore didn't look

close enough, she kept tellin' him she
had this lump in her breast... I'm
alright... She's got a three-month-
old kid and she's come home to die...
Thing is no one's got around to tellin'
her that's how it is. They asked me
to come over and tell her...patients
of mine...come home to die...

> (OSCAR may exit. Pause. EV takes
> Gramma's letter out of his pocket
> and looks at it)

EV: I'm alright...

> (Shift)

BOB: Open it! Go on, open it!

EV: You're drunk.

BOB: I'm drunk. So I'm drunk. What the
           hell are you, what's your excuse?
           What's his excuse, Katie?

EV: Leave her alone.

BOB: Why don't you open it!

EV: What for?

BOB: To see what it says.

EV: Says nothing.

BOB: Your father's mother killed herself,
           Katie. She walked across the train
           bridge at midnight and -

KATIE: That's an accident!

BOB: She left a letter and the letter tells
            him why she did it.

KATIE: What's in the letter, Daddy?

EV: Your Gramma--

            (OSCAR may unobtrusively enter,
            and stand silently in the
            background)

BOB: She killed herself because of him!

KATIE: Because of you!

EV: Your Gramma loved us.

KATIE: Why don't you open it?

EV: She didn't see us so she'd write.

BOB: So open it!

EV: That's all it is.

BOB: Pretending! He's pretending!

KATIE: He is not!

BOB: He pretends a lot!

KATIE: You do!

BOB: Valma! Valma! Valma!

KATIE: I hate you!

BOB: Not afraid to say it!

KATIE: I hate you and I wish that you were
            dead!

CATHERINE: No.

KATIE: It's true!

CATHERINE: No.

KATIE: I wish and wish and

CATHERINE: No.

KATIE: someday you will be dead and I'll
be happy!

OSCAR: It's all right, Katie!

KATIE: (to EV) You all say she's sick, she
isn't sick.

BOB: (to KATIE) Katie!

KATIE: She's a drunk and that's what we should
say!

BOB: (to CATHERINE) Katie!?

CATHERINE: Stop.

KATIE: And if I find her next time, I won't
call for Daddy!

CATHERINE: No.

KATIE: I won't call for anyone!

CATHERINE: Stop Katie please.

KATIE: (sits) I'll go back downstairs and
I'll sit in the kitchen and I'll
pretend that I don't know, I'll
pretend that everything's all right,
I'll shut my eyes, and I'll pretend!

BOB: Katie! (retreats)

KATIE: (chants) Now they're married wish
            them joy

BOB: Katie. (exits)

KATIE: (puts hands over ears; chants louder)
            First a girl for a toy
            Seven years after seven to come

BOB: (voice-over on mike, offstage) Katie!

KATIE: (chants louder) Fire on the mountain,
                kiss and run
            on the mountains berries sweet

BOB: (on mike, offstage) Katie!

KATIE: (chants) Pick as much as you can eat
            By the berries' bitter bark

BOB: (on mike, offstage) Katie!

KATIE: (chants louder) Fire on the mountain
                break your heart
            Years to come - kiss and run
            bitter bark - break your heart

            (KATIE slowly takes her hands
              from her ears. There is silence.
            Pause)

            I don't hear you! (pause) I don't
            hear you! (pause) I don't!

            (KATIE jumps up and whirls around,
              to look over at where she last
              saw BOB. Pause)

KATIE: (softly) I don't hear you at all.

CATHERINE: You can cry, Katie...it's all right to cry...

KATIE: Would you want to have me?

CATHERINE: Yes, yes I would.

(Shift)

EV: All over now.

(EV gets up from chair and moves to the table where CATHERINE left the jewellery box in Act One. He stands, looking down at it)

CATHERINE: No, Daddy.

OSCAR: When was it we played scrub hockey on the river ice... Ev and Oscar, Oscar, Ev... "We're rough, we're tough, we're from Devon, that's enough"...

(EV lifts the lid of the music box. It plays "Smoke Gets In Your Eyes")

...driving my old man's car, watering his whiskey, Ev and Oscar...

EV: Ever since Grade One.

OSCAR: I knew you then, and I knew you after that, and then I got to know you less and less - and here we are... I said why risk it? And I saw her and I knew

why...well, she's gone now... What
the hell does that mean to you, Ev.
That's something I want to know.
What's it mean?... For Christ's sake,
say something, say anything.

EV: There's nothing to say.

OSCAR: It shouldn't have happened.

EV: It did. (closes the music box)

OSCAR: She asked for goddamn little and you
couldn't even give her that.

EV: You got no more idea of what she wanted
than I have.

OSCAR: You never knew her and you don't know
me.

EV: How can you say that? I carried you
on my back since Grade One cause I
liked you, I loved you, like a brother.

OSCAR: I could see it in my father, I can see
it in you. You got your eye fixed on
some goddamn horizon, and while you're
striding towards that, you trample on
every goddamn thing around you!

EV: The biggest dream you ever had, what
the hell was it? What was it, Oscar?
New Orleans! New Orleans.

OSCAR: She understood what that meant.

EV: Bullshit. You been a pseudo-doctor
for your old man, a pseudo-husband to
my wife, and a pseudo-father to my

kids! I gave you that, Oscar, like
I gave you everything else cause I
knew you'd never have the goddamn
gumption to get it for yourself!

OSCAR: I should have taken your wife.

EV: My wife wouldn't have you!

           (OSCAR starts to leave. EV
           calls after him)

She knew you! She knew what you were!
And because of that you say I killed
her! It was all my fault?

           (OSCAR stops. EV moves to him)

Supposin' it were, her death my fault,
put a figure on it, eh? Her death my
fault on one side - and the other any
old figure, thousand lives the figure -
was that worth it?

           (OSCAR exits)

Was it? I'm askin' you a question! Was
that worth it!

           (Silence. Shift. KATIE approaches
           EV. As he removes his suitcoat,
           he speaks to her)

What the hell do you mean?

KATIE: I don't know what I mean.

EV: Where the hell would you go?

KATIE: I don't know. Away. Away to some school.

EV: I don't want you to go.

KATIE: Send me anyway. For me, Daddy. Do it for me.

EV: What if I said no.

KATIE: You won't say no.

EV: You wanna hear me say no!

KATIE: I'm like you, Daddy. I just gotta win - and you just gotta win - and if you say no - you'll have lost. (exiting as she speaks) I'll come back...every once in a while...I'll come back...

EV: Katie? (screams) Katie!

CATHERINE: I'm here.

(Shift. CATHERINE and EV are alone onstage. As CATHERINE speaks, EV puts on his old cardigan, which was hanging on the back of his chair. He puts on his glasses. CATHERINE has Gramma's letter)

Do you remember when she gathered together all the photographs and snapshots, all the pictures of her, and she sat in the living room, and she ripped them all up? So...after she died, we had no pictures of her... And Oscar, remember Oscar came over with one...it was taken at a nightclub somewhere, and she was feeding this little pig - a stupid little pig standing on the table and she - she was feeding it with a little bottle like a baby's bottle...

EV: Her with...

CATHERINE: ...a baby bottle feeding the pig with the bottle...

EV: (small chuckle) Her and Oscar at some god-damn Caribbean nightclub feedin' a pig...

CATHERINE: Like a baby. She was looking up at the camera. She was smiling a bit. You could see her teeth. She didn't look happy, or unhappy. She looked as if she was waiting. Just waiting.

EV: For what?

CATHERINE: I don't know. But whatever it was, she couldn't grab it.

EV: Do you know what you want?

CATHERINE: ...Yes ...Yes, I do.

EV: Then you grab it.

CATHERINE: (Pause; looks at Gramma's letter, which she is holding in her hand) What are you gonna do with this?

EV: Do you wanna open it?

CATHERINE: I can. Do you want me to?

EV: I know what's in it.

(Pause. CATHERINE strikes a match. She looks at EV)

CATHERINE: Should I?...should I?...

                    (CATHERINE blows the match out
                    and gives the letter to EV. He
                    sits looking at it for a moment)

EV: Burn the goddamn thing.

                    (EV holds the letter out.
                    CATHERINE sets it on fire and
                    it flares up as EV holds it)

CATHERINE: Be careful!

EV: I am bein' careful.

                    (EV drops the burning envelope
                    into an ashtray. Lights are
                    fading)

             Two minutes home you're as bad as
             Valma.

CATHERINE: Bullshit, Daddy.

EV: Jesus Christ I hate to hear a woman
             talk like that.

                    As lights fade to black,
                    CATHERINE looks at EV and
                    smiles. Black except for the
                    dying flame from the letter.

                    The End